Powerful Evangelism
for the Powerless

Powerful Evangelism for the Powerless

A new, revised edition of
Evangelism and Your Church

C. John Miller

P&R
PUBLISHING
P.O. BOX 817 • PHILLIPSBURG • NEW JERSEY 08865-0817

Originally
Evangelism and Your Church
©1980 C. John Miller

Revised edition
Powerful Evangelism for the Powerless
©1997 by Rose Marie Miller

Unless otherwise indicated, Scripture quotations are from the author's
translation or from the Authorized Version. Italics indicate emphasis
added.

Composition by Colophon Typesetting

Printed in the United States of America

Library of Congress Cataloging-in-Publication Data

Miller, C. John.
    Powerful evangelism for the powerless / C. John Miller. — Rev. ed.
        p.   cm.
    Rev. ed. of: Evangelism and your church. 1980.
    Includes bibliographical references.
    ISBN 0-87552-383-8
    1. Witness bearing (Christianity).   2. Evangelistic work.
I. Miller, C. John.   Evangelism and your church.   II. Title.
BV4520.M553   1997
269'.2—dc21   97-6827

Contents

Revitalizing the Passive in America

EARLY IN THE TWENTIETH CENTURY, Baptist evangelists preached through rural Mississippi and Alabama with such effectiveness that moonshiners could no longer sell their whiskey: All their customers were getting converted! In desperation, the whiskey sellers hired two men to murder one of the leading Baptist preachers.

Pistols in their hands, the assassins waited in the dark outside a country church where their target was preaching. The evangelist spoke with burning intensity about heaven and hell, his voice ringing out into the night. When everyone had gone, he turned out the church lights and stepped outside. The killers approached him, pistols in hand.

But instead of shooting the evangelist, they handed him their guns. "We came here to kill you, but we couldn't," they said. "We heard your preaching and we believed it. We're now on the same side."

Evangelize or Perish!

That story was told to me years ago by a pastor in Alabama. The Baptist evangelist was his grandfather. The story stayed with me. It is compelling drama and a parable of our position in an increasingly dangerous and demoralized world. Either we evan-

1

gelize our generation with new power or its members are going to kill us. The bad guys are waiting for us "out there" and intend to do us in. It is no longer a case of choosing or rejecting the evangelistic option. It's the *only* option. Every daily newspaper in America carries on its pages the story that we (and our world) are in a position of immediate peril. We need an evangelism with enough strength to get the bad guys before they get us.

Dr. Paul Long, Sr., professor of missions at Reformed Theological Seminary, urged me a number of times to have this out-of-print book republished because it stresses finding a vision of grace so big that it will cause us to give up churchly passivity for bold witnessing activity. I somewhat reluctantly agreed to attempt the revision. The publisher was enthusiastic, but still, it took a number of newspaper articles in the *Philadelphia Inquirer* to shake me awake to the urgent need for a more powerful evangelism.

The Need of the Hour

George F. Will wrote a column (May 30, 1991) calling for "a cohort of contemporary Wesleys" to revitalize the nonworking urban poor in our time. He reasoned that liberal governmental policies have created a climate of dependency among many of the poor of our cities. Consequently, they are becoming nonworkers—not because of lack of opportunity but because they are demoralized. Will concluded that a city like New York does not need more social help programs; instead, "it needs John Wesley" to revitalize the passive poor.

Will called for an army of contemporary Wesleys to revitalize "the passive in America." Predictably, the letters to newspapers around the country reflected the anguish of secular humanists over Will's bombshell. How dare he suggest that deprived people needed old-time religion more than they needed more government intervention!

At about the same time, David R. Boldt, then senior editor of the *Inquirer's* editorial page, called for "a Third Great Awakening in America." He followed up that daring call for spiritual revival with a response to Will's earlier column. Boldt critiqued Will for not emphasizing "sufficiently the need for a restoration of religious values *throughout* American society." He also personalized the spiritual need. Boldt said that revival must begin with each of us taking a "look in the mirror." When Boldt looked at himself, he saw that his own face was "corroded by cynicism and doubt."

We are deeply challenged by these honest attempts to identify the core elements in a religious awakening. On the public side, we are asked to consider the need for Wesley-type spiritual leaders with enough fire in the belly to turn masses of people from depravity to dignity. On the personal side, we are invited to look in the mirror to discover how much depravity needs to be confronted in ourselves as a first step toward a new "Great Awakening."

Admitting one's flaws is often the first step toward correction. As evangelicals we must begin by admitting that, with some exceptions, we are not "a cohort of Wesleys," and we are certainly not a cohort of George Whitefields and Tennents, the people who led the Great Awakening in the Philadelphia area. Actually, we may be nicer people. We don't tell archbishops in public that they need to be born again (Whitefield) or read out in church a list of local pastors needing conversion (Gilbert Tennent in Nottingham, Pennsylvania). At the same time, we lack their compelling faith, astonishing courage, and compassionate risk-taking. Clearly these men were the instruments of a divine working. Through grace they were humble men who spoke with irresistible authority about heaven and hell.

Boldt challenged us to begin the New Great Awakening by looking at ourselves in the mirror. My suggestion is that we use the examples of the leaders of the first Great Awakening as our mirror. Here are three ways in which they differ from us.

Key #1: Confidence in Christ's Authority

Evangelism is always a frightening, painful, delightful, wonderful enterprise. There is something deeply personal about it.

And that personal element makes it difficult to express what goes into it. But I am convinced that what gave evangelists in the eighteenth century remarkable power was the Whitefield-Wesley confidence in the supreme authority of Christ. Jesus acted in and through them not because they were powerful persons, but because they were empty vessels needing grace. He was the one who forgave and cleansed them; He was the one who sent them with the gospel; and He was the one who opened the hearts of hardened people to a very humbling message.

By contrast, believers today typically serve a much smaller Christ. We like His role of comforter and sustainer, but we pretty much ignore His royal position as the conquering King. His command to evangelize the world (the Great Commission) is seen as optional, and when we read it that way, we soon end up wondering why we have become so self-absorbed and joyless. The sad fact is that we are often more aware of human opinion than we are of Christ's claim to have absolute authority over the whole cosmos ("All authority in heaven and earth has been given me." [Matt. 28:18]).

Here is our basic failure. Without conscious submission to Christ's supreme authority, today's pastors and church leaders have generally given up the right of spiritual inquiry into the state of the human soul. In fact, no one even uses the term "soul" any longer. When we respond to human crisis, we much prefer the more impersonal and sometimes de-Christianized vocabulary of the professional counselor or therapist, Christian or otherwise.

The leaders of the Great Awakening had extraordinary power in evangelism and renewal. They followed an omnipotent Christ, the divine warrior, and He anointed them with His missionary presence. But this power was poured out on those who knew that they were inherently powerless without a constant dependence upon the working of God's grace in their lives. They knew themselves as poor sinners.

This knowledge was not crippling. Awareness of depravity humbled their natural arrogance. John Wesley may have been naturally one of the proudest men who ever lived. But once aware of his flawed nature, he hungered for God. Such men grew into giants on the earth. Though once they were crippled by guilt, Christ cleansed and healed them. He had spoken an authoritative, compelling word of forgiveness to their souls. So, of course, they knew that He could speak the same word of forgiving grace to others through their preaching. God had done great things for them; He could do great things for others.

Key #2: Confidence in the Whole Truth

Today we aim to get people to make "a decision for Christ" with as much speed and as little pain as possible. We may then encourage these persons never to doubt their salvation. But in our well-meaning haste we may deceive ourselves and those we are trying to evangelize. Often we do not take the trouble to explain to people that "choosing Christ" is not an act of human autonomy but a *surrender* of human autonomy. We often teach them little about God and His perfect righteousness and His demand that we be perfectly righteous ourselves. We minimize original sin and our deeply rooted self-will. We soft-pedal hell.

This is what is most serious: We then fail to find out the actual spiritual state of our hearers. We act as if we are afraid to offend them. No wonder somewhere between 40 and 50 million Americans profess to be born again, with many of them deeply confused about what it even means. Think of the confusion frequently created by our shallow evangelistic invitations. We tell people that God loves them and Christ died for them and leave them to wonder why His love is all that great, since we did not challenge their notion that they are pretty good folks. Forgiven little, they love little (Luke 7:47).

Trevor McIlwaine, a missionary with New Tribes Mission, tells the story of his wife's aunt, who went forward in an evangelistic service. She was later asked, "Aunty, why did you go forward to the invitation of the preacher? Was it because you realized you were a sinner?"

Her reply was, "A sinner? I'm not a sinner!"

By contrast, renewal preachers like Whitefield and the Tennents faced their hearers with the biblical truth about their lost condition. They labored hard to make their hearers understand that the majestic Christ demands more than a religious experience or even a surface moral reform; He requires a changed inner life in the new birth and conversion. Furthermore, they did not call a religious experience conversion unless spiritual fruit accompanied the profession of faith.

Key #3: A Passion for Winning Souls

Christians often have two levels of belief and do not recognize it. They have official concepts in their minds that are fully biblical, but deep down they may have another belief system that contradicts the correct teachings. For instance, we evangelicals usually "believe in hell," but it is not part of our daily working theology. Sometimes this lack of sensitivity to eternal judgment is due to pure apathy. We literally "don't give a damn for the damned." Seen in a more sympathetic light, some of us may simply be trying to avoid putting off church visitors who need some pre-evangelism in a user-friendly setting. But even here the danger is that our methodology will become one that controls, unconsciously, our theology, so that compassion for the hell-bound fades from our minds.

What we see is that our evangelical ancestors were soldiers, whereas we tend to think and act like civilians. These eighteenth-century evangelists thought deeply about eternal issues, prayed with intense fervor, worked harder than anyone else, and outfought the gin sellers (the eighteenth-century version of crack dealers). They were God's "soul winners," soldiers marching in God's army of love. I doubt very much that it ever occurred to them that "winning souls" might limit divine sovereignty or suggest psychological manipulation. To reach the consciences of his hearers, John Wesley preached in Dublin, Ireland, with an empty coffin at his side. When Whitefield preached to the stubborn miners of Bristol, he wept in prayer with a great outpouring of tears for their lostness. Soon his surging concern broke their hearts and their coal-stained faces were streaked white with their own tears.

What we learn from their example is that the passive in America—and perhaps in the rest of the world—are not just the nonworking urban poor. To quote Pogo, "We have met the enemy, and he is us." We, the passive evangelicals, are all too often among the nonworking civilians. To echo John Piper's *The Pleasures of God, we have gone AWOL.*

THE ORIGINAL VERSION OF THIS BOOK bore the title *Evangelism and Your Church*. That content is substantially unaltered. I have, however, spotlighted with new intensity the theme of evangelism as a call to war. In sharpening this vision, I have revised some of the chapters, added new ones, inserted quotations for meditation between chapters, and added study questions and exercises at the end of each chapter. I have also broadened the application of the material, seeking to make it relevant to denominations beyond the circle of my Reformed theological tradition.

I have changed the title to *Powerful Evangelism for the Powerless*. The play on John Wimber's *Power Evangelism* is obvious, but I intend no disrespect. My concern, rather, is to expose the hidden root of an evangelism that has a biblical militancy. I want to show that the root of our powerlessness must go deep into the soil of grace. As we go with the gospel, our part is to discover His strength in the presence of our incapacity. It is that combination of our weakness claiming His strength that causes "the word of grace to run and be glorified" (2 Thess. 3:1–2).

Years ago when I was first working on this book, I told Leda Herron, a good friend of mine, that I was troubled by my lack of faith in the power of the gospel. Ironically I confessed my weakness to her at a time when many people in our church were making professions of faith in Christ. The church was filled with praise in spite of my sense of my limitations. A good soul doctor, Leda asked me, "Didn't one of the Moravians tell Wesley to preach faith until he had faith? Maybe you should do that."

She added with a smile, "Preach faith until you are full of faith, and then do your evangelism as though you were full of faith no matter how you feel."

I did what she said. In fear and trembling I went with the gospel to a number of lawless people. Some of those people were powerfully changed by Christ's message and are now leaders in the Christian church. The glory is entirely God's, who is willing to use soldiers who often go AWOL in their hearts. Be encouraged by this. If His grace can use me, then certainly He can use you.

ONE

The Unspent Treasure: Our Missionary Legacy

Do you remember "Roots?" Few things captured the imagination of the American public so completely as that first television mini-series, a chronicle of a black family's life. All of a sudden, people were scouring archives and attics for traces of their own family history. Overnight, the past became the "latest thing." It was seen by thousands of Americans as the key to a deeper sense of personal identity.

I don't believe that the American public had ever experienced a phenomenon quite like "Roots," but it wasn't the first time that I had seen large groups of people delve into the past with great curiosity and enthusiasm. As a pastor, seminary teacher, and church planter during the past thirty years, I have seen that an interest in theological roots runs deep among Christians of almost every tradition. My own origins lie within the circle of Reformed and Presbyterian churches. There I have observed many times that retelling the story of our Reformation heritage will light up countenances as little else can! Our historical roots are very important to us.

And really, isn't that as it should be? The events that spread the gospel through Western Europe should inspire doxologies in the person who loves God's Word. Our forefather John Calvin, in particular, is justly honored as a scholar, pastor, and teacher who embodied the Reformation commitment to a faith governed by the Word of God.

In my opinion, the Reformed community would be hard to surpass in the way it has respected and preserved its historical and spiritual heritage. And yet one thing about our secular, "Roots"-seeking counterparts has challenged me regarding the manner in which we study our past. Above all other considerations, the secular seekers' interest in their pasts is supremely *practical*. They study their family histories because they believe that such knowledge will provide them with a perspective that will enable them to function better *today*. They are convinced that the past will open the door to the present, that it will help them to find perspective and purpose now.

Most of us would agree that these individuals are expecting too much from an assemblage of historical data. It is unrealistic to believe that one's past history will infuse meaning and purpose into a life that otherwise lacks them. As Christians, however, our position is different. Our individual and corporate lives *do* have meaning and purpose: to glorify God through the faithful ministry of the gospel of His Son, as it is contained in the Scriptures. We know why we are here; we do not need to look to the past to find that answer. However, I am convinced that a study of our religious heritage could be of immense instrumental value if we sought from it practical insights on the ministries of men like Calvin, Knox, Whitefield, and Edwards. What was their understanding of their ministries? How did their perspectives shape the form their works took? What elements of their perspectives and priorities may we adapt to our twenty-first–century ministry?

We as believers need to ask questions like that today, because most of us would agree that the Reformed community, along with the broader evangelical church, has lost much of the impact it had on the world in other periods since the Reformation. It seems as if we are heirs to a vast spiritual inheritance, but we don't know what to do with it. We know it is valuable, so we guard it to keep it intact. But we lack the practical wisdom to take our fortune and reinvest it, so that the treasures of the past may yield new bounty in our generation.

A number of facts about present-day evangelical and Reformed Christianity suggest that we have not fully "invested" our spiritual inheritance. Consider what we see within some of our churches. Something has gone wrong when a friendly visitor attends one of our urban churches and comes out saying, as one did, "I agreed with the theology of the sermon, but the whole service carried the odor of death." Some notable exceptions in our tradition have occurred recently in the U.S. and throughout the world. For example, the Presbyterian Church in America has engaged in vigorous church planting in North America and throughout the world. But even in this denomination, what Louie M. Barnes, Jr., wrote in the seventies still has relevance for many congregations. He said that "the average local church in the U.S." has "barely one nostril out of the water," with Reformed churches in most cases "experiencing the same nosedive in 'growth' rates."[1] With even more burning passion, Sam Moffet, veteran missionary strategist, says that contemporary Christian religious communities (including all denominations) have a "ghetto complex" that segregates them from non-Christians and makes effective evangelism extremely difficult.

What is the fundamental cause of this self-containment and consequent evangelistic barrenness?

As I have studied our forefathers—mine as well as those in the Anglican, Baptist, Methodist, Plymouth Brethren, and Moravian traditions—I cannot escape a disturbing conclusion: we have lost their deep conviction that the gospel, the Word of God, is *alive* and *active,* a message so powerful and so thoroughly irresistible when applied by the Holy Spirit, that it could not help but bear fruit in the salvation of souls. Their reverence for the Word and for the doctrines of grace was great, just as ours is today, but the difference between us is this: While our emphasis is on preserving true doctrine and defending the faith, theirs was on taking the gospel and going on the offensive, bringing God's message to men and conquering them in Christ. They wanted not only to preserve the gospel, but to put it to work, to see it change lives and expand God's kingdom.

Baptist Charles Haddon Spurgeon's ministry illustrates the perspective I am describing. The source of power for his preaching can be seen in this sermon excerpt:

> Oh, the power, the melting, conquering, transforming power of that dear cross of Christ! My brethren, we have but to abide by the preaching of it, we have but constantly to tell abroad the matchless story, and we may expect to see the most remarkable spiritual results. We need despair of no man now that Jesus has died for sinners. With such a hammer as the doctrine of the cross, the most flinty heart will be broken; and with such a fire as the sweet love of Christ, the most mighty iceberg will be melted. We need never despair for the heathenish or superstitious races of men; if we can but find occasion to bring the doctrine of Christ crucified into contact with their natures, it will yet change them, and Christ will be their king.[2]

It was said of Anglican George Whitefield (by no less a preacher than John Newton) that "he never preached in vain."[3] J. C. Ryle describes him as "the first to see that Christ's ministers must do the work of fishermen. They must not wait for souls to come to them, but must go after souls, and 'compel them to come in.' "[4]

What was his motivation? "Cry out who will against this my frowardness," wrote Whitefield, "I cannot see my dear countrymen, and fellow Christians everywhere ready to perish through ignorance and unbelief, and not endeavor to convince them of both."[5] And to what did Whitefield attribute the amazing fruit of his preaching? "I intend to exalt and contend for more and more," he once wrote of his future ministry; "not with carnal weapons—that be far from me—but with the sword of the Spirit, the Word of God! No sword like that!"[6]

Calvin also felt the divine imperative not merely to defend the gospel, but to preach it actively to men. In his commentary on John 4:34, he notes,

> The nature of Christ's office is well known—to advance the Kingdom of God, to restore lost souls to life, to spread the light of the Gospel and in short to bring salvation to the world. The importance of these things made Him forget meat and drink when He was tired and hungry. From this we receive no common comfort. It tells us that Christ was so anxious for men's salvation that the height of pleasure for Him was to attend to it; for we cannot doubt that He has the same attitude towards us today.[7]

What is common to these quotations, and to the men of faith who wrote them, is the deep awareness of God's foremost intention for His Word and for the church to whom it is entrusted: It is intended to glorify His great name *in its orientation toward the salvation of the lost!*

God had a missionary purpose when He gave mankind His Word. His desire to reveal Himself to men pervades Scripture from Genesis to Revelation (Gen. 3:15; Rev. 22:17). The fervor of men like Calvin, Whitefield, Spurgeon, Knox, Edwards, and Newton to reach out to the world with the gospel came because by faith they embraced that purpose as their own. This is what we need to learn from our forebears; indeed, this is what we need to learn from God Himself.

We need to come to grips with God's missionary purpose for His Word. John Newton once commented that "Calvinism was one of the worst of systems preached theoretically, but one of the best preached practically."[8] I fear that many pastors today have fallen into the error of preaching the doctrines of grace theoretically instead of preaching them practically and using the truths of Scripture to draw men to Christ. Instead of using the Bible as our instrument to draw men into fellowship with God, biblical doctrine has become our grounds to exclude those—even other believers—who disagree with us. Instead of using the Scripture as the sword of the Spirit to conquer men for Christ, we spend our energies defending it, as if it were fragile and easily broken.

I do not wish to dismiss the church's responsibility to guard her sheep from wolves teaching false doctrine. My problem lies solely with the assumption that such concerns must have first place in the normal ministry of the church. This protectiveness overturns God's standard order for the church and its ministry. God's first priority for His church is to proclaim the gospel to the lost, bringing them to salvation. This is followed by the cultivation of the life and unity which that gospel produces among Christ's people. And finally, in that context, as a living testimony to the power of the Word, the church defends herself against error.

It is noteworthy that Calvin did not suffer from the reversal of priorities from which we suffer. Calvin knew the Bible as a great missionary book in a way that few moderns do. For him it was largely a book of promises centering on Christ's conquest of the nations through gospel preaching. This can be seen in his commentary on Isaiah 2:3, where he says that men out of "all nations" will be conquered by "the doctrines of the gospel" and stream to Christ. Commenting on the verse that follows, he adds,

> By these words he first declares that the godly will be filled with such an ardent desire to spread the doctrines of religion, that every one not satisfied with his own calling and his personal knowledge will desire to draw others along with him. And nothing could be more inconsistent with the nature of faith than that deadness which would lead a man to disregard his brethren, and to keep the light of knowledge choked up within his own breast.[9]

Calvin was not slow to translate his own missionary vision into action. During the years 1555 to 1562, eighty-eight men were trained and commissioned by Calvin as pastors to France. Additional works established in Holland and Scotland by men trained by Calvin were greatly blessed. In Scotland, the response to Christ was so overwhelming that one contemporary observed that "the sky rained men."

In Germany, England, Wales, Poland, and Hungary, flourishing evangelical Presbyterian and Reformed churches were planted and strengthened by men trained in Geneva. Even such ardently Catholic lands as Italy and Spain were touched by their influence. An amazing zeal for Christ's cause and God's glory were instilled in the men Calvin taught.

Yet somewhere in the years between Calvin's century and ours, our working theology has become abbreviated in a way that would have dismayed such a pioneer in missions. Our emphasis on the wonderful doctrines of grace has somehow come to mask and perhaps (in our own minds) even justify a deep-seated indifference to the lost. Evangelism, God's first priority for His Word and His church, has become a peripheral activity in the lives of many local congregations. Often it even raises eyebrows as a theologically questionable undertaking because it is so far afield of our usual defensive posture! Louie Barnes noted this attitude in his aforementioned report. Unlike other denominational leaders whose church rolls were shrinking, Barnes observed that Reformed churchmen "sense very little urgency in this matter." In fact, he says, "many of my colleagues believe that a rapidly expanding, active 'church' is proof positive that doctrinal or ethical compromise has certainly taken place."[10]

I also have observed this attitude among my Reformed contacts. I recall an incident in which one man in a Reformed setting accused another of Arminianism. Asked to justify his charge, he replied simply, "He does aggressive evangelism; that means he's Arminian." In another instance, a Reformed pastor was alarmed that Campus Crusade for Christ had come through his community and motivated many of his people to witness in shopping malls. His response was to teach a class in which he "proved" that church officers alone were intended to do evangelism.

Of course, these are extreme examples. But what concerns me is their roots in a widely held conviction that evangelistic zeal is suspect. The inadequacies of some evangelistic groups may fuel those feelings, but I firmly believe that the greatest reason for our antipathy to zeal is that we have overlooked God's oft-affirmed intention to draw the lost to Himself through the proclamation of His Word.

If God's primary commitment to reveal Himself to the world is as clear as I have maintained, why have so many well-trained, godly, and dedicated pastors missed it? I attribute this myopia to a "remnant theology" that makes the idea of aggressive evangelism seem pointless. One pastor defended the position this way: "We must not be impatient with history. This is the day of small things; apostasy has reduced us to a remnant. We should really rejoice that ours is the privilege of purifying and strengthening these few."

But a theology of fewness has no meaning for God's people since the event of Pentecost. Such a small vision simply does not square with the finality of Peter's bold announcement that the "last days" have come and that an age of fullness has dawned, with the Spirit being poured out abundantly "upon all flesh" (Acts 2:17). Today we have the banquet of abundant grace! We must open the eyes of faith to the wonder of God's saving purpose, reaching out since Pentecost to embrace the nations. Our faith must be a fighting faith that takes into account the global promises of Isaiah, Ezekiel, Zechariah, John, and Luke, which began to be fulfilled at Pentecost.

If we as witnessing Christian communities are to regain our strength, we need to recover a biblical theology of expectancy founded upon the knowledge that the sovereignty of God is not restricted to the salvation of a few individuals. Scripture clearly connects it to God's saving purpose as it relates to all the world, as evidenced in His own missionary character, as sealed in His promises, and as defined by His gift of all authority to the Son as the conquering Lord of the Great Commission. Scripture's great message to human beings is the offer of abundant life in Jesus Christ, and God's revealed intention is for many to hear the message and be saved. My purpose in this book is to outline the biblical basis for a theology of missionary expectancy and to suggest practical ways in which courageous faith based on such a theology may revitalize our churches.

Faith Understands God's Missionary Character

It is easy to say the words to myself "God loves me" and to tell others "God loves you." But a realistic knowledge of God's righteousness and our own unrighteousness makes it difficult to believe that God loves us as we really are. We know from the Scriptures that God hates sin. Our minds reflect our anxiety over our unworthiness by filling up with negative images about God, ourselves, and other people. How then shall we know He loves us and others except by faith? And if faith is to have life in it, it must have biblical content. Faith can only grow strong by seeing that our missionary hope is founded in God's unchangeable commitment to glorify Himself by bringing to Himself people from all nations.

Faith, then, builds on what Scripture says about God's missionary character.

From the beginning of biblical revelation, God makes it clear that He has a missionary burden for mankind. When Adam and Eve fled His presence after the Fall, He called them to faith and repentance with the promise that their seed would be His people, and would someday produce a victor who would crush Satan's head (Gen. 3:15). We learn early, too, that God is a jealous God (Ex. 20:1–6; Deut. 4). In the first commandment He declares that He alone is God, and in the second commandment that He cannot bear that the devotion He deserves be given to graven images. The God who reveals Himself in the second commandment is a missionary God who cannot rest until He has established a knowledge of Himself in every corner of the earth (Ex. 20:4–6; Deut. 4:23–24; Isa. 42:1–8; Num. 14:21; Isa. 6:3; 11:9; 40:5; Hab. 2:14). His message to the nations is, "I am the LORD, that is my name; my glory I will not give to another, nor my praise to graven images" (Isa. 42:8 NASB).

Sensitive to the nature of the second commandment, Jesus cleansed the temple at the beginning and close of His public ministry (John 2:13–22; Matt. 21:12–13). He understood that the new age had come and that the court of the Gentiles (where the vendors and moneychangers had assembled) must be purged so that the nations might draw near to God. The temple was being readied by its Lord to become a house of prayer for all peoples (Isa. 56:6–8; John 2:13–22).

This desire of God's to reveal Himself stems from His nature as an inexhaustible fountain of life. His immortality (or life) is not the endless, cold existence of Aristotle's Unmoved Mover, but a superabounding personal life, an immortality of boundless vitality, overflowing love, and creative delight (1 Tim. 1:17; 6:15–16). The astonishing fullness of physical life found in the earth, the air, and the seas is eloquent testimony to God's nature (Gen. 1; Ps. 104). He is fullness of life and He delights in life (John 1:1–16). And though He hates all sin, He has no pleasure in the death of the wicked (Ezek. 33:11). The God who passionately seeks the glory of His own name also desires to impart His fullness of life to human beings everywhere (John 1:4; 5:26).

In John 4, we see more clearly how God's zeal for His own worship and His divine delight in imparting life come together. Here Jesus identifies the Father as the Great Missionary. He asks us to believe that He is seeking true worshipers among the wicked and alien of the earth (vv. 2–3, 16–18). He seeks their worship but He also imparts to them through the Son a spiritual life described as "a spring of water" that is nothing less than the Holy Spirit shed forth at Pentecost by the exalted Lord Jesus (Acts 2:33; John 7:37–39).

Faith Appropriates God's Missionary Promises

Christ's advent is the ultimate expression of the Father's desire to reveal Himself to men (John 1:18). In His Son, the Father makes it clear to our faith that He is formally and totally committed to rescuing the nations from the bondage of sin and Satan, and turning vast multitudes into followers of the Lamb (Gen. 12:3; Gal. 3:8; Matt. 28:16–20). What is more, the Bible stimulates our faith in Christ's work by expressing it in the form of trustworthy promises. God promises to bring the fullness of Christ's life to mankind and to fill the world with His glory through the ministry of Christ's Spirit (Isa. 44:1–5; Joel

2:28–30; John 4:14; 7:37–39; 10:10; 15:1–11). In particular, these Christ-centered promises inspire us with the confidence that the harvest is plenteous (Luke 10:1–2), that the elect are a multitude that no man can number (Rev. 7:9), and that the cross reveals a saving mercy which confronts all men everywhere with God's desire for their salvation (John 3:16–17; 1 Tim. 1:15; 2:4–6).

It is this promised saving mercy that faith must appropriate. It must do so daringly if it is to grow bold, loving, and self-forgetting.

Following Christ into the harvest field is not an enterprise for the faint-hearted or the half-persuaded. We need the strongest assurance that our work is not self-generated, but that our believing is hooked into what God is doing in history. That is why God has revealed Himself to us in Scripture as the sovereign missionary. But to strengthen our convictions further, the Lord has expressed His missionary concern in the form of great promises of grace. These promises mean that God has bound Himself to do certain things by commitments that are stronger than steel and yet kinder than a mother's love. In brief, these promises assure us of the omnipotence of God's grace. They also invite us to believe and know how very dear to Him are sinners of all kinds and races.

These promises come to us—and to all the world—with astonishing winsomeness in the Gospel of John. Calvin sums it all up in his comments on John 3:16. Note his gladness as he says, "The word *only begotten* is emphasized to praise the fervor of the divine love toward us. For men are not easily convinced that God loves them; . . . to remove all doubt, He has expressly stated that we are so very dear to God that for our sakes He did not spare even His only begotten Son."[11]

Faith Follows the Lord of the Great Commission

These world-embracing promises have special significance for the church, for they all flow from the person and work of Christ as triumphant Lord of the Great Commission. As has often been noted, the Great Commission is Christ's missionary command directed to His body, but it is also an announcement of

Christ's sovereign conquest of the whole earth. It expresses His intention to claim every inch of it for the honor of the triune God. The Great Commission issues from Christ's conquest of all creation at the cross and the tomb, where He earned the right to all authority in heaven and earth (Matt. 28:18; Rom. 1:4; Acts 2:33–36), including the right to equip every believer with a Spirit of witness (John 15:26; 20:21–22).

Today the Great Commission is seen in a variety of confused ways: as a bare legal command unrelated to grace; optional advice not to be taken seriously by busy Christians; and as an imperative directed primarily, if not exclusively, to official missionaries.

Such views of the Lord's missionary command isolate the Great Commission from its connection with the Old Testament and its stress upon the Son of Man as the absolute ruler, the King of grace. From Daniel 7 we learn that this mysterious figure will conquer every square inch of this world and eliminate all idolatrous, competing religions. The Great Commission is the Lord's Great Declaration of War. In it, the triumphant Son of Man calls the whole church to abandon civilian status and put itself upon a wartime footing.

Thus the Great Commission must be seen as having three primary connections.

The Absolute Kingly Authority of the Son of Man

This authority is prophesied in Daniel 7:13–14 and Psalms 2 and 110. It is fulfilled in the atoning sacrifice and resurrection of our Lord. Using almost the exact words of Daniel 7:14, Jesus says, "All authority in heaven and earth has been given to me" (Matt. 28:18). Here in the Great Commission He presents to our faith His sovereign right and intention to conquer all competing authorities and persons (Phil. 2:9–11; Rev. 19–21).

The war is on!

His Defeat of Satan's Authority at the Cross

We go with the gospel to the nations only because of Jesus' destruction of Satan's legal authority over the world. So the Great

Commission is connected to Jesus' defeat of Satan by His atonement (Col. 1:13–14; 2:14–15; Rev. 12:10–12). We witness with sure confidence, knowing that the Accuser and his demons are defeated enemies. The powers of evil fight with terrible intensity a battle that has already been lost, whereas believers by grace fight with humble boldness a battle that has already been won.

The Gift of the Loving Authority of the Son of Man

Here are three connecting words the Christian church should never forget: "Just as" and "also." They occur in the form of the Great Commission given in the Gospel of John. "*Just as* the Father has sent forth me, I *also* send you" (John 20:21). The church is not a continuing incarnation of the Son of Man, but it is indwelt by His missionary Spirit and has His continuing mission of tender love. We go into the harvest with the legal authority and the powerful presence of the risen Lord. We are a commissioned church, touched by His heart for the lost (John 17:18; Matt. 28:20; Acts 1:2).

Practical Conclusions

There are numerous practical implications of these truths for our faith. First, they give us faith for the conflict arising from Christ's authority. To paraphrase John Calvin's comment on Matthew 28:18: No ordinary authority would here have been enough, but sovereign and truly divine government ought to be possessed by Him who commands them to promise eternal life in His name, to reduce the whole world under His sway, and to publish a doctrine that subdues all pride.[12]

Second, our faith is strengthened to embrace the church's identity: That is, the prime mission of the church is missions. As I note elsewhere, "What we are calling for is a rethinking of the Great Commission, to read it so as to see that it is defining the church in the most radical terms. The missionary mandate is not simply . . . to send missionaries into the harvest field. It certainly is that. But the entire church is a 'sent church,' a commissioned body that is itself involved in the harvesting task."[13]

Moreover, "When the church goes with the gospel, it is not

man's will being carried out. The church is out there reporting a divine summons from the throne. The gospel messengers are announcing that the Lord of the harvest is on His way, and now is the hour to surrender to His salvation in faith and repentance."[14]

Finally, Christ's authority deepens our faith to sign up for the gospel fight, the holy war, and leave behind the civilian life. We accept our identity and calling as members of the church who are sent ones, pilgrim-soldiers, led of the Spirit in triumph.

"The Church is the pilgrim people of God. It is on the move— hastening to the ends of the earth to beseech all men to be reconciled to God, and hastening to the end of time to meet its Lord who will gather all into one."[15]

Harvie Conn has pointed out that "one cannot be a missionary church and continue insisting that the world must come to the church on the church's terms. It must become a 'go' structure. And it can do that only when its concerns are directed outside itself toward the poor, the abused, and the oppressed. The church must recapture its identity as the only organization in the world that exists for the sake of its nonmembers."[16]

In summary then, the Great Commission is both an announcement of the binding victory over sin and Satan won at the cross (Col. 2:13–15) and a call for each of us to give up civilian status and follow Christ with a holy disregard of personal cost (John 12:23–33)! The Great Commission is God's declaration of war. His Christ is the divine warrior leading us into the last battle (Pss. 2; 110; Dan. 7; Rev. 5:7–10; 7:9–14; 11:15–19; 12:10–12; 15:1–4; 20:1–15). That last battle involves the whole conflict of Christ with Satan, but its center is the struggle to take the gospel to all nations before His final appearing (Mark 13:10).

Missionary harvest and conflict go together. We are the sons and daughters of God through faith, and as God's children we must go to the work with sickle and sword. As we go with the gospel, we will hear the two words that Jesus spoke to His disciples: "Fear not."

The fruitfulness of His work—and His call for us to participate in it with fearlessness—is anticipated by Jesus' first commissioning of His disciples at the Sea of Galilee. By their own efforts they had fished all night and taken nothing. But at Jesus' command, they took a mighty draught of fish, so that their "nets were breaking" (Luke 5:6 RSV). In this setting, Jesus announces, "Do not be afraid; henceforth you will be catching men" (Luke 5:10 RSV). The sign becomes a parable, then, of the kingdom harvest and the courageous faith of the witnessing church (Luke 10:1–2; John 4:35; 12:32).

By faith we expect rich harvest fields and breaking nets, for the gospel is specifically designed to bear fruit. It is the "word of truth, the gospel," which bears fruit among the Colossians, "as indeed in the whole world it is bearing fruit and growing" (Col. 1:6 RSV). In Acts we discover that the Word of the living Lord conquers sinners in Jerusalem and the priests in the temple (6:7), nullifies man's eloquence (12:20–24), subdues the Gentiles (13:48–49), and reduces man's magic to ashes (19:17–20). His gospel conquers three thousand men at Pentecost, with five thousand more converted shortly thereafter, and makes the book of Acts to be what someone has called the New Testament book of Numbers because of its recording of the great numbers of conversions (6:7; 9:31, 42; 11:21, 24, 26; 12:24; 14:1, 21; 16:5; 19:20).

Our brief summary reveals that the God of the Scriptures has a passionate commitment to evangelism—His mighty, holy heart is in it all the way. Pentecost was God's graphic announcement that His saving intentions were now to be applied to the church and the world. The victory of the Lord over sin and death led to a "new birth" for the church as it was seized by God's own missionary purpose. In the words of Herman Bavinck, "On that day this church is born as mission church and world church."[17]

Obviously, then, we are living out of touch with what God is doing in the age of the Spirit if we have no zeal for witness. We have become detached from roots much deeper than those that tie us to Calvin: we have cut ourselves off from the purpose of the Christian church since its inception. For this coldness we must repent and confess this sin particularly. Each pastor reading this chapter needs to own up to any sermons that were preached without concern for the lost and did not reflect any of God's saving purpose for men, to the failure to pray for unsaved hearers, to the forgetting of unsaved visitors coming to Lord's Day worship. Elders who do not labor full time in the Word also need to ask themselves about priorities. How often their lives fall into patterns of such busyness or rigidity that they do not have time to witness! They find themselves reserving their zeal for their own affairs rather than God's purpose for the world.

Our hope for renewed vitality in our Christian communities rests on our willingness to expand our vision and align our faith with God's sovereign missionary purposes throughout the world. We need to ask Him to send His Spirit to instruct us on how to go with the gospel in a spirit of confident expectancy, rooted in His promises and the fullness of the working of the Holy Spirit. This believing expectancy is most crucial. Our participation in God's great world harvest initiated at Pentecost is founded in faith, and faith without expectancy is an empty shell, mere mental assent which means nothing before God. But faith filled with humble confidence in God's character and promises is the mark of the kingdom's presence and power. From this assurance comes a singleness of mind, a determination to get the gospel to men no matter what the cost.

Finding the Cutting Edge

1. State the purpose of this book in one sentence.
2. What is "a remnant theology"? How does that compare with a "theology of biblical expectancy"?
3. Explain in one paragraph the following statement: "The God of the Scriptures has a passionate commitment to evangelism—His mighty, holy heart is in it all the way."
4. Identify your own commitment to evangelism. Circle the appropriate number: (1) none, (2) a little, (3) sometimes, (4) often, (5) passionate/constant.
5. If your response is 3 or less, consider how much God loves you. Read John 3:14–17, and meditate on Calvin's brief comment on verse 16: "The word 'only begotten' is emphasized

to praise the fervor of the divine love toward us. For men are not easily convinced that God loves them . . . to remove all doubt, He has expressly stated that we are so very dear to God that for our sakes He did not spare even His only begotten Son." Note the words "the fervor of the divine love." Apply them to yourself and then extend them to all the world.

6. The cutting edge of grace: You are not trying to create your love for human beings by your own will power. Instead, in simple faith ask the Father to take you into "the fervor of the divine love" for people who are lost.

Notes

1. Louie M. Barnes, Jr., *The Church and Her Ministry* (Pittsburgh: The Board of Education and Publication, Reformed Church of North America, 1976), 53.

2. Charles Haddon Spurgeon, *The Passion and Death of Christ* (Grand Rapids: Eerdmans, 1970), 45.

3. J. C. Ryle, *Select Sermons of George Whitefield* (London: Banner of Truth, 1958), 30.

4. Ibid., 31.

5. Arnold Dallimore, *George Whitefield, Volume I* (London: Banner of Truth, 1970), 338.

6. Ibid., 409.

7. John Calvin, *Calvin's Commentary, The Gospel According to St. John,* trans. T. H. L. Parker (Grand Rapids: Eerdmans, 1959), 1:105–6.

8. *The Autobiography of William Jay,* ed. George Redford and John Angell James (London: Banner of Truth, 1974), 569.

9. John Calvin, *Calvin's Commentaries, Commentary on Isaiah* (Grand Rapids: Eerdmans, 1948), 1:94.

10. Barnes, *Church and Her Ministry,* 53.

11. Calvin, *Gospel According to St. John,* 4:74.

12. John Calvin, *Calvin's Commentaries, Matthew, Mark and Luke* (Grand Rapids, Eerdmans, 1975), 3:249.

13. C. John Miller, *Outgrowing the Ingrown Church* (Grand Rapids: Zondervan, 1986), 52–53.

14. Ibid., 55.

15. Lesslie Newbigin, *The Household of God* (New York: Friendship Press, 1954), 18.

16. Harvie M. Conn, *Evangelism: Doing Justice and Preaching Grace* (Grand Rapids: Zondervan, 1982; Phillipsburg, N.J.: Presbyterian and Reformed, 1992), 23.

17. Herman Bavinck, *Our Reasonable Faith,* trans. Henry Zylstra (Grand Rapids: Eerdmans, 1956), 390.

This sense of having been sent was a fundamental awareness of Jesus. It gave significance, urgency, and compulsion to everything he did. . . . If God was to Jesus, "he who sent me," then Jesus must be to us, "he who sent us. . ." The church is the community of Jesus who have first been chosen out of the world and then sent back into the world. . . . In order to qualify for the name "church" <u>we must be a community deeply and constantly aware of</u> our "sentness," and actively loyal to this part of our Christian identity.

—JOHN STOTT,
"THE LORD CHRIST IS
A MISSIONARY CHRIST"

TWO

How Big Is God's Mission Field?

A LOOK AT THE UNIVERSE reveals that God has a certain style: the massive and the majestic. God's workings in the spiritual realm follow the same pattern. It should not surprise us that the prophet Isaiah would refer to the coming of the Messiah as a "strange deed," a work so earthshaking in magnitude that it would sweep away all evil and lay the foundation for a whole new order (Isa. 28:14–33; 52:13–53:12).

That is exactly what happened at the cross. It was not the place where, as Albert Schweitzer once concluded, Jesus was crushed by the wheel of history, but rather where the Son of Man took that wheel and reversed its whole direction.

At Calvary the demon powers lost their authority over the world (Col. 1:13; 2:15), the guilt of sin was canceled (Col. 2:13–14), sonship was conferred upon all who believe (John 1:12), and the Holy Spirit was purchased for the life and sanctification of the church (John 1:29, 33; 7:37–39). God offers no tiny gospel. It is a work so great that no man can remain neutral before it. "And I," says Jesus, "if I be lifted up from the earth will draw all men unto me" (John 12:32).

The dimensions of God's deed of salvation should challenge us, convict us, and encourage us in our evangelism. Yet, as we saw in the previous chapter, many Christians, particularly those with Reformed convictions, act as if God's work at Calvary was very small. Their belief that God elects those who will be

27

saved has led them too often to the unconscious assumption that the cross concerns only a few, and that the wisdom of offering it to the rest is questionable.

This is no minor snarl in our theology. In fact, I am persuaded that misconceptions here have led many Reformed pastors virtually to eliminate the gospel from their preaching. And though most of them would formally reject hyper-Calvinism as much as Arminianism, there is substantial evidence that they often preach and teach as if they believed it. At the very least, they do not offer the cross to men with believable conviction or with pointed application to their hearts.

This criticism is not meant to minimize the importance of the doctrine of election. We are right to believe that Christ died with saving efficacy for His sheep alone. You cannot escape the particularity of great passages like John 10:15, where Jesus tenderly and emphatically announces His great love for His own people. The Lord means for us to understand that He really purchased salvation for His people and irresistibly applies it to their hearts. He did not buy them a hypothetical salvation or atone for the sins of all men.

But we make a great mistake if we think this is the whole story. It is an important part—indeed, it is the foundational part—but it should not be understood in a way that wipes out the reality of the free offer of the gospel and prevents the preacher or witnessing Christian from aiming the gospel directly at people. The particular design of the atonement must not be permitted to cancel out related biblical teaching that the cross is sincerely offered to all persons everywhere.

God's saving purpose has a bearing upon all sinners in this world. "For God," says the Gospel of John, "did not send the Son into the world to condemn the world, but that the world might be saved through Him" (John 3:17). Paul says, "It is a reliable saying, deserving full acceptance, that Christ Jesus came into the world to save sinners, among whom I am the foremost" (1 Tim. 1:15). He adds in the same letter that "God our Savior . . . desires all men to be saved and to come to the knowledge of the truth" (2:3–4 NASB).

From these passages we see that the primary goal of God's sending His Son to the world was not to condemn but to save. His concern was clearly to bring salvation to a mankind under eternal condemnation. In the cross God faced us all with His astonishing deed of love. In the terse words of John Calvin, "The Heavenly Father does not wish the human race that He loves to perish."[1]

A study of John 3:16 helps to bring this truth to sharper focus. It seems obvious that this verse does not teach the Arminian view that Christ died with a saving efficacy for everyone, including Judas. It also should be clear that John 3:16 is not saying the same thing as John 10:15, where Jesus speaks about laying down His life for His sheep. What it says is that the gift of the Son by the Father represents His astounding love for all mankind. It is talking about the cross as God's supreme deed of loving confrontation with an evil world, and the cross as God's invitation to every man to receive this salvation by faith.

In a great sermon entitled "God's Immeasurable Love,"[2] B. B. Warfield argues that "the world" in John 3:16 does not refer to the whole of mankind as I have suggested, but to the evil *in* mankind. In effect, he believed that the elect are in view as a "world" of depraved sinners, and hence the term "world" refers not to the whole race but to the sin of man in its intensity and depth.

The church is indebted to Warfield for spotlighting the awfulness of human depravity conveyed by the term "the world," but this does not prove that the "world" here can be limited to the elect. It takes a good deal of scholarly sophistication to draw such a conclusion from the text, and, even more importantly, the thematic emphasis of the passage does not fall on the design of the atonement for the elect, but on the greatness of the gift and its saving effect on all those who respond to the invitation in faith. What comes through to the reader is the Father's love in the matchless gift of His Son, so that whoever appropriates this gift is granted eternal life as a present possession. John 3:16 does not close the door on anyone. It spells out the invitational character of verses 14–15, which had climaxed with a statement of God's purpose to save *"whoever* believes in Him,"

William Hendriksen takes up this point in his commentary on this great verse. He writes,

> God does not leave mankind to itself. He so loved the world that his Son, the only begotten, he gave, with *this purpose:* that those who receive him with *abiding trust and confidence* may have *everlasting life.* Though the Gospel is proclaimed to men of every tribe and nation, not every one who hears it believes in the Son. But *whoever believes*—whether he be a Jew or a Gentile—has everlasting life.[3]

The universal character of God's offer in John 3:16 is also reinforced by the parallelism between "the world" and the race of men in the immediate context. In verse 19, for instance, we read, "And this is the condemnation, that the light has come into *the world,* and that *men* loved darkness rather than the light; for their deeds were evil." It appears inescapable that here "the world" and lost "men" or mankind are one and the same.

In short, what we discover in John 3:14–21 and the rest of the Gospel of John is that the covenant of grace has come to a world-embracing fulfillment. Centuries before, God had promised this to Abraham when He said, "In you all the families of the earth shall bless themselves" (Gen. 12:3; Gal. 3:8). In the gift of His Son the Father has wondrously fulfilled this global promise. The world, with its terrible hostility to God, is now invited to embrace this love. This invitational theme with its universal offer is announced at the beginning of this Gospel (1:7), forms the context for John 3:16 (3:14–15), and controls the use of major images in the book such as water, bread, and "lifting up" (i.e., the cross).

Yet too many Reformed scholars have ignored these promises because their view of election does not really permit such a free and open gospel invitation. I believe that the text requires our affirmation of an indiscriminate offer of the gospel to men;

but, whether you agree or not, you do need to see that a biblical doctrine like the definite atonement must not be permitted to silence the offer of the gospel or to leave it abstract and vague. <u>The Christian who witnesses needs to know that God loves the world with a holy passion.</u> We must be fully confident that God is really sincere in His love to wicked men, and that He desires our salvation with a most compassionate heart.

With R. B. Kuiper, we must let John 3:16 grip us. In his words, "John 3:16 makes the amazing, incomprehensible, unfathomably profound, well nigh unbelievable, declaration that the holy God sovereignly loves hell-deserving sinners, and that he loves them so much that he was willing that his only begotten Son, whom he loves with all the love of his infinite heart, should go to hell in their stead."[4]

If our witness does not reflect that burning conviction, our offer of the cross easily becomes a hollow charade. Our theology slips into a barren moralism and legalism. It weakens our own consciousness of our majestic God's infinite love and it leaves our hearers in unbelief and confusion. Our house of doctrine has walls, roof, and foundation, but it has no door by which faith may enter. The offer of the cross is the only way of access to God. Take that away and the sinner has no basis for hope, and every other doctrine will come across to him as burdensome law, hard and unsympathetic, with grace nothing but a bare word without content. But show him Christ, his door of access, and then he knows the way to go in and out and find rich pasture. As Calvin said, "We must hold up this shield, that God does not want us to be overwhelmed in everlasting destruction, for He has ordained His Son to be the salvation of the world."[5]

But many evangelical pastors seem to have an *unconscious* alienation from a biblical theology of the cross. I know of a pastor who rarely preaches the gospel to his congregation, even though each Sunday almost one-fourth of the several hundred people who attend are visitors or nonmembers. But he preaches <u>discipleship without an atonement.</u> I wish to be kind, but that is a moralistic message, misleading for Christians and leaving unbelievers at eternal risk. Somehow this man has lost touch with his own sinfulness and the ongoing necessity of his own cleansing by Jesus' blood.

Any pastor who cannot connect discipleship and Calvary has a life and a ministry that are drifting into Pharisaism. As a practical measure the preacher who consistently omits the message of the cross from his sermons should take a long break from ministry and simply sit with John 3:14–21 till it catches fire in the mind and life.

The heart of the matter is that preaching, like personal witnessing, is an instrument of war, and we must approach the task with that kind of seriousness.

After ten years of ministry, the implications of this for my preaching and witnessing became clear to me. Until that time I had never seen anyone converted through my pulpit ministry. I began to read the sermons of Charles Spurgeon, Walter Maier, and Martyn Lloyd-Jones. I also studied the messages in the book of Acts. Almost immediately I learned from the messages of men like Spurgeon that they knew how to summarize the gospel quickly and to point sinners directly to Christ. Along with this, I discovered that these men and the apostolic heralds in Acts preached to me in the second person. Sometimes they used "we" as one sinner speaking to another, but at the point of confrontation they took aim at particular men and said "you."

This startled me. My preaching had often been earnest, but it had been third person or first person exclusively—never a direct exhortation to come to Christ. But once I made the matter one of special prayer, almost immediately two people responded to the exhortation and showed evidence of new life. I had the same experience meeting people on a one-to-one basis. I began to ask, "Do you know personally about the love of God? Do you love Jesus because He died at Calvary for the sins of men?"

I had learned a great lesson: If you want to see people saved, it is your duty to aim the gospel directly at them. This is true of preaching from the pulpit; it is equally true of the use of an evangelistic booklet like "A New Life."[6]

Yet this leaves an important question unanswered. How does this offer of the cross relate to doctrines like unconditional election and particular atonement?

I suspect we often labor to force an artificial harmony between different lines of biblical teaching; nonetheless, God's truth *does* have a harmony. While a missionary to Korea, Harvie Conn resolved this apparent tension beautifully in his evangelism of prostitutes of his city. He began a Bible study on Ephesians 1, sharing with these women the truth of an electing love that creates vessels of holiness for God. The stress fell on what God has done in Christ to beautify the undeserving, a message of special poignancy to those involved in deep sexual sin.

It was not long before one of these wretched women would ask, "How can I have anything to do with this? You talk about holy lives that Christ is building, but that couldn't happen to me. I have fallen too far into sin."

The missionary made it clear that it is not what we do but what God has done in Christ to elect, purchase, and apply a salvation that matters. Then the question inevitably came: "How can I get this salvation?"

In response, the missionary took these despairing women to Ephesians 2:8–10 to show that faith is the way by which one enters into salvation. He would say something like this: "You are right to despair of ever being able to make yourself into a child of God. But if you put your trust in the Lord Jesus, you will be united to Him. You can then be sure that the Father elected you to holiness in Him before the foundation of the world, that Jesus died to save you eternally, and that the Spirit has forever sealed your salvation."

At the close of the final Bible study, Mr. Conn called on the women to follow him out the door of the brothel and run for their lives. "They were all held by chains of guilt," he said later, "but those who were persuaded that mercy and grace were meant for them ran."

This is the main point of this chapter. Sinners only run to Christ when they are persuaded that mercy is available to them. Our fears of "easy believism" and of "cheap grace" ought not to lead us to think that we should preach a hard discipleship which excludes sinners from mercy. This missionary rightly saw that each biblical doctrine should be presented in a way that preserves its evangelical character and shows sinners that grace is immediately available for every contrite heart.

Such an approach also unveils the underlying harmony between the preaching of Christ's death as a universal invitation and the truths of election and the definite atonement. The cross is offered indiscriminately to all who hear. God is sincere in this compassionate offer. At the same time, the universal call is made even more personal by teaching the hearer that Christ died with a special, irresistible design for His own sheep and that the hearer can know that he is one of them by trusting his life to Christ.

The free offer of the gospel and the particular doctrines of sovereign grace are great friends. Do not make them enemies. Let them build your confidence in God's love for you, and then share with sinners the wonder of God's love manifested on a hill outside Jerusalem.

Finding the Cutting Edge

1. What is the primary goal in God's sending His Son into the world?
2. What reasons are given in this chapter for thinking that John 3:16 does not refer to the elect but to all mankind?
3. Is it then biblical to say, "God loves you and sent His Son to bring you eternal life"? If you disagree, develop your own formulation.
4. Complete this sentence: "I discovered that these men and the apostolic heralds in Acts preached to me . . ." What is the significance of this kind of preaching? If you are a pastor, do you preach this way?
5. How did the missionary to Korea resolve the apparent tension between election (God's choice of the child of God) and a person's responsibility to repent and believe (to take grace into your own life)?

6. The cutting edge of grace: Think of someone you know who is in bondage to guilt and shame. Then write him or her a letter explaining about grace that is big enough to take it all away.

Notes

1. John Calvin, *Calvin's Commentaries, The Gospel According to St. John,* trans. T. H. L. Parker (Grand Rapids: Eerdmans, 1959), 1:73.

2. B. B. Warfield, "God's Immeasurable Love," *Biblical and Theological Studies* (Philadelphia: Presbyterian and Reformed, 1952), 505–22.

3. William Hendriksen, *New Testament Commentary, Exposition of the Gospel of John,* 2 vols. (Grand Rapids: Baker, 1953), 1:141.

4. R. B. Kuiper, *God-Centered Evangelism: A Presentation of the Scriptural Theology of Evangelism* (Grand Rapids: Baker, 1961), 25.

5. Calvin, *Gospel According to St. John,* 75.

6. The purpose and use of the "New Life" booklet is explained in chapter 13 of this volume.

*God has chosen the Church,
we who are His believing people,
to be the sole agents through whom
His love and grace will reach the
lost world. . . . Paramount on the
Church's agenda is the concern of
"communicating Christ to the world."*

—PHILIP MOHABIR,
WORLDS WITHIN REACH

THREE

How Deep Is God's Love?

WE HAVE BEEN EXAMINING truths that have given many Christians a zeal for witness that they never had before. I believe that God has few delights greater than to see His children go out with the gospel, confident of His commitment to evangelism and His promise of a harvest of barn-bursting proportions.

Yet we all know that it takes more than a formal knowledge of these things to motivate a believer to share his faith with the lost. Too many of us know horror stories about well-catechized churches that failed woefully in their witness to the unsaved. A pastor from a West Coast town remembers the night a man who had never been to church walked through the doors of a conservative church. The idea of visiting a church had so unnerved the man that he had taken several shots of whiskey to fortify his courage, and when he seated himself in the congregation, the unmistakable odor of drink wafted through the air around him. As his nearest neighbors sniffed in dismay, each one of them silently got up and moved.

"The man was left sitting in an empty circle. No one sat nearer than a dozen feet of him in any direction," the pastor recalled. "Understandably, he never returned. There was no chance to give him the gospel."

I don't know about you, but my first reaction to that story was to hope that such an attitude toward the world's "unwashed" was confined to that one unfortunate congregation. But, lest we reproach one church unfairly, we need to ask ourselves if things would have gone much differently had the incident taken place in *our* churches. Can we say with confidence that we would have welcomed him? Had him home for supper? Put him up for the night? Given him money? Committed ourselves to extended counseling?

Only God can tell us truly how we have responded to the strangers He has sent into our midst. We may have done better than we think, or worse. But the Holy Spirit does convict us of sin for the times we have responded to a needy person with fear or a sense of alienation. God has called His church to be a welcoming church, to stand as His representatives on earth and welcome *everyone* to His heavenly banquet. He wants the love and compassion of the gospel to be heard from our lips. If we find ourselves unable to offer that welcome, to speak that message of love, to seek out those who need it, God wants us to realize something is wrong.

Well, yes, we concede, we can see that something is wrong. We need to pray for more zeal, more love, more boldness, more of a servant's heart, we say. But, no, God says, you are missing something even more basic. How do you respond instinctively to the outsider, the drunkard, the adulterer, or the drug addict? First, with fear for your physical safety, or for a schedule that may be irreparably disrupted if you become involved with such a person? And you also respond with a superior attitude—the feeling that this is someone with whom you have nothing in common, an alien creature who needs help in a way you never have. You think—perhaps unconsciously—that the gap that separates you in society places you in different categories with God as well. But that, says God, is where you are wrong. And this may be the root of your problem with evangelism: you don't understand the gospel—for yourself or anyone else! You are an insider, "tight" with the right people, and, you hope, with God.

There are many professing Christians who have never fully grasped how lost in sin they really were, and how low God had to stoop to save them. The propriety and morality of their outward lives has made it hard for them to believe that their need to be redeemed was as desperate as anyone else's. Up to a point, they are convinced of their need for salvation, but the fact that their outward lives have been unmarked by scandal or blasphemy has caused them to feel as if they don't need it *quite as much* as some other people they see.

This complacent attitude toward the gospel, unarticulated though it may be, has two chief effects on the believer. The first is a distance between himself and God that, somehow, he is never able to overcome. He doesn't understand why; he believes the right things, he prays, he is active in church and is willing to serve. But the problem came about when he first placed himself partially out of the reach of the gospel and of grace. A person who has limited his need for God's grace has inevitably limited his relationship with God. God's unconditional, unlimited love for him is something he has missed. It is beyond the realm of his self-centered experience. He doesn't, at bottom, really understand what happened—for him—at the cross. He feels a need for many things, but does not hunger for the grace of atonement. And it is very likely that the gap he senses in his relationship with God is causing him either to try to earn God's favor with good works, or to rationalize away the richness of other Christian lives as maudlin, pietistic, or imbalanced.

It is easy to see that the second effect of such an attitude toward the gospel concerns the believer's relationship to the lost. A person who has not heard God's words of compassion himself as a lost person cannot communicate them to others. If, in our own minds, we have limited our need for the gospel, we will hardly identify with sinners in obvious need of saving grace. We feel removed from them, just as we feel removed from the full impact of the gospel. We don't understand that we, too, were and are allied to the "unwashed" when God met us with the gospel. The distance we feel from both the message and those who need to hear it soon disengages us altogether from the enterprise of evangelism. Salvation? Well, it is God's covenant commitment to forgive, we say to ourselves, reducing the magnitude of God's work to match our shallow experience of it. It will get done somehow. And the world? Well, it's pretty obvious that if those "unwashed" out there were really sincere about the gospel, they would clean up and get to work. Then we'd be willing to witness to them.

With many members in this frame of mind, what soon evolves is an inward-looking church that exists for her own sake. God seems far away, and so do the lost, so the highest goal becomes the congregation's own comfort, order, and safety. Protected from the outside world by walls of elaborate doctrine or self-contained worship, the church is never challenged about the spiritual void that threatens to consume her, because non-Christians can seldom make their way inside!

What a tragedy! And how hard it is to admit that it may be so with us! But our living Lord Jesus has powerful medicine to heal His church, if she is willing to acknowledge her need. That medicine is the gospel as it really is, not as we have truncated it by our unbelief. We can be healed of our sins by learning afresh from the Holy Spirit about the riches of the message of Christ (Col. 2:9–10). Let us examine again some of the crucial points of the gospel message that we may have missed.

Paul defines the gospel as the "good news" or "good message" that "Christ died for our sins according to the scriptures; and that he was buried, and that he rose again the third day according to the scriptures" (1 Cor. 15:3–4). What confronts us in Paul's summary is a cross, i.e., a substitutionary atonement, and "our sins." The two belong together. The cross represents God's assessment of the seriousness of our sin, and it is only when we see this that we can comprehend the fullness of grace displayed in the atonement, God's provision for the sins of His elect. A true perception of these two spiritual facts—the gravity of our sin, and the infinite depth of God's grace revealed in the cross—is what we need most as Christians to make the message of grace a transforming reality within us.

Those of us, especially, who have been spared a lurid past can gain a truer understanding of our profound need for the cross by considering our obligations to God as summarized in the first commandment: "You shall have no other gods before Me" (Ex. 20:3 NKJV). The intent is not that God is to be put first, while all other things are to take second place. Rather, the commandment announces that God alone is God; there can be no second or third places for anyone or anything. Literally, the idea is that "You shall have no other gods in my sight" or "before my face."

This unyielding command requires complete surrender to God of all that I am and have. Do I own my house? My car? My family? My religious attainments? Not really. I am only a steward of God's gifts. All that I have is to be immediately and completely at His disposal. Asaph caught the meaning when he cried, "Whom have I in heaven but You? And there is none upon earth that I desire besides You. My flesh and my heart fail; but God is the strength of my heart and my portion forever" (Ps. 73:25–26 NKJV).

Jesus phrased it like this when asked what was the greatest or first commandment: "The first of all the commandments is: 'Hear, O Israel, the LORD our God, the LORD is one. And you shall love the LORD your God with all your heart, with all your soul, with all your mind, and with all your strength' " (Mark 12:29–30 NKJV).

The first commandment is the foundation for all the others. It puts the "fear" or worship of God at the center of every "ought" in the divine law. It means that in keeping each of the other nine commandments, we must give up self-preoccupation and return our heart's adoration to the living God. In keeping the sixth commandment, for example, I must not kill my neighbor in thought, word, or deed. I must set aside prejudices against him and self-righteous attitudes of superiority toward him. Where he has wronged me, I must forgive him. I must devote myself to furthering his welfare as though his life were my own. And in doing all this, I am required to act out of devotion to the God who has made us both.

The God-centered character of the law makes plain the extent to which every human being has fallen short of its holy requirements. When we face the law's exalted nature, we begin to understand, for example, that our present-day consumerism is more than "keeping up with the Joneses": it is rebellion against the Most High. It is taking His property and treating it as though it were our own by inherent right. As a habitual action it can only be described as a course of practical atheism. An overstatement? Not to God. I am by nature, therefore, the just object of God's wrath. I am part of that "world" addressed in John 3:16 just as much as any drunkard or adulterer. I may not have the odor of whiskey on my breath, but is not the smell of my self-righteousness much more offensive to God?

Until we face our condemnation before the law and acknowledge our conceit and spiritual rebellion, too many of us Christians feel superior to the world's more conspicuous sinners, while blinded to the greatness of God's love to sinners at the cross. But if we take the first commandment in the manner God intended, we are *all* exposed as worldly to the core. We "clean-living" sinners are no less fallen that anyone else. It is the nature we have received from Adam that condemns us, and our own self-centered habits reveal our kinship with our fallen father.

Yet the first commandment also brilliantly illuminates the means of our healing; it makes clear why the Father so freely and righteously accepts the work of His Son in our behalf.

The answer lies in the righteous quality of the Son's obedience. Eternally equal with the Father, the Son was commissioned by Him to take on our human nature and live and die in our place. This was an obedience of complete humiliation characterized by an exciting word—willingness. In the light of His own performance, the Son could say, "I delight to do your will, O my God. Your law is in my heart" (Ps. 40:8); "I have no other gods before you" (Matt. 4:10). It was His obedience to the first commandment that delighted the Father and required that He accept the Son's atonement as a matter of perfect justice (Phil. 2:1–11; Eph. 5:1–2). The Father in turn rejoiced that at last one man stood on the center of the stage of history who could say truthfully, "I love the Lord with all my heart and with all my soul and with all my strength and with all my mind."

Now we sense something of the depth of God's passionate love at the cross. In the person of His Son, the Highest came down to save the lowest and lift us up to be with Him. His justice required that He dip the being of His only begotten Son into the depths of hell for our sakes. As Thomas Kelly wrote,

> *Many hands were raised to wound Him,*
> *None would interpose to save;*
> *But the deepest stroke that pierced Him*
> *Was the stroke that justice gave.*[1]

We should expect that a confrontation between the God of the first commandment and us worldlings would unleash holy wrath upon us. But instead of a curse, we are staggered by the massiveness of God's love.

Perhaps it seems strange to direct what is essentially evangelistic material to an audience concerned about mobilizing other believers to evangelize. But Scripture teaches that not everyone who claims to be part of God's people is really one of God's own (Matt. 7:21–27). Mere profession proves little if it is not accompanied by life change. Several years ago, a good friend of mine took a problem-ridden congregation as his first pastorate. For him to have exhorted the people to evangelism would have made little sense because he quickly saw signs that many of them were themselves not converted. He quietly embarked on a visitation program to evangelize each family, and before many months had passed, he saw over sixty couples turned to Christ.

There are other reasons, too, that I emphasize the gospel to those who say they already believe it. Many of our church members may have been born again, but their knowledge of their sin and the grace of God is so shallow that, in a real way, they need the message of salvation to come into their hearts with something very like first-time conversion. And there is also a sense in which even more mature believers must confess that the world and the love of material comforts are too much with them. We quickly grow cold and self-sufficient.

The first commandment continuously reveals that I have an unlimited need for a reconciling Savior. Though I have passed from condemnation to pardon once and for all, and have been legally adopted as God's son or daughter, my sanctification *also* depends on my daily coming to Christ as a saved sinner (1 John 1:8–26). God's gift of faith does more than effect my union with Christ by justification. Faith is also the Spirit's means to bring me back to Christ again and again for cleansing and filling at the fountain of life (Heb. 10:19–22; Rom. 6; Ps. 51).[2] True faith always has a hungry mouth for the bread that does not perish.

Apart from a soul hunger for Christ there is no cure for the religious professionalism and lukewarmness that forever crouches at the door of the self-satisfied Christian. A friend summed up the issue like this: "When I first became a Christian, I was a poor beggar telling other poor beggars where to find bread. Gradually, though, I became an *ex*-beggar telling poor beggars to find bread." When our witnessing sinks to this level, we seek not to win others by our welcoming love, but to protect ourselves from any deep involvement in their lives.

The truth is that in our heart of hearts, we all long to be "ex-beggars," self-sufficient, capable human beings, straightening out other people from above. But grace does not work that way. It falls on the fallen, the needy, the broken, and the guilty. We have it most abundantly when we raise crippled, bleeding hands to heaven, crying out for help that we know we cannot provide for ourselves.

God never intended to save us from our sins so that we would go on to accomplish our sanctification in our own strength, and witness out of this proud accomplishment. Instead, His Holy Spirit convicts believers of sin so that we will be drawn to the God of John 3:16 and the forgiveness available in His Son. A daily awareness that we must never stray from Calvary ourselves is the most important element in a God-honoring evangelism. As I experience the gospel as a message of a righteous God's total forgiveness, and Christ as the magnetic, personal center of my life, evangelizing with a gospel of forgiveness is a natural and inevitable outgrowth. It breaks down my blinding pride; it reminds me of what our God of love has done for me. And so it is, then, that we find ourselves truly able to help someone like the whiskey-drinking visitor. What we offer to him is not social discipline, which excludes him before he has an opportunity to hear about a reconciling Christ. Rather, having been humbled ourselves by our own present need, we approach the lost person with a new welcoming attitude. We have no desire to encourage him to continue in his sin, but to invite him to join us in going to Christ for total renewal. We want him to see with us the breadth and depth of the law of God as governed by the first commandment and then to experience the power of Jesus' blood to cleanse us and to write God's law in our inmost being.

Approaching witness from this comprehensive point of view, we leaders can bring a fresh awareness of healing grace to our ministries. We will not be trying to train our people in something alien to them and to us. Personal witness and evangelism as an enterprise will issue from our delight in God and the appreciation of His grace in Jesus Christ. We will be able to receive strangers as friends, so that they may experience through us the welcoming attitude of Christ.

Finding the Cutting Edge

1. Why do you think the church members moved away from the man smelling of whiskey?
2. How do you respond instinctively to the following kinds of people?
   a. A teenager with bad manners?
   b. Someone in your family or church who committed adultery?
   c. A drunk or drug addict?
   d. A self-righteous friend or relative who judges you severely?
   e. A member of another race, social class, or tribe who does strange things?

3. What is often missing when we react without compassion and wisdom?
4. How does the law break pride and self-righteousness? How does the message of the cross overwhelm our prejudices with the greatness of God's self-giving love?
5. The cutting edge of grace: Memorize a hymn that summarizes the big idea in this chapter and then sing it to yourself as you meet different kinds of people.

Notes

1. Quoted from Thomas Kelly's hymn, "Stricken, Smitten, and Afflicted," Selection 192, *Trinity Hymnal* (Philadelphia: Orthodox Presbyterian Church, 1961).

2. Cf. John Murray, *Redemption Accomplished and Applied* (Grand Rapids: Eerdmans, 1955), 116. In this context, Murray is speaking primarily of repentance, but what he says of repentance also applies to faith in its ongoing relationship to a living Christ. He says, "Christ's blood is the layer of initial cleansing but it is also the fountain to which the believer must continually repair."

Just as the Spirit came upon Jesus to equip him for his public ministry, so now the Spirit was to come upon his people to equip them for theirs. . . . He would impel them to proclaim throughout the world the good news of His salvation. Salvation is given to be shared.

—JOHN STOTT,
THE SPIRIT, THE CHURCH,
AND THE WORLD

FOUR

The Marks of Biblical Boldness

WE HAVE BEEN TALKING about God's total commitment to evangelism, the love He displayed to all men in the gospel offer, the high cost of Christ's redemptive victory, and the triumphant advance of God's kingdom through our obedience to Christ's missionary command. Much more could be said about all of these things, but without their practical application to the life of the believer, the battle for evangelism will be lost before it begins. Fear and confusion about the work of evangelism so often diminish the impact these truths ought to have on our faith and our witness.

I recall a young convert named Tom who exemplified the struggle of many Christians. He confided, "I find it so hard to witness. I try to analyze all the things I should say, but I freeze up when I should speak up. I can see a big struggle ahead in overcoming my fears."

That need not be the case if Tom is taught to take seriously the new identity he has in Christ. Legally, he has been adopted into the family of God (John 1:12). Morally, he has received the nature of the Son of God through a new birth which preceded his legal adoption (John 1:13). He has passed from death to life in becoming the Father's child (1 John 3:1–14). He is a living, holy son of God caught up in a program of worldwide redemptive conquest (Matt. 28:16–20).

Tom, as well as every other believer, has this new identity because the Spirit of Christ now lives and works in him. And this new identity inevitably leads him to a life of witness because the Spirit has been commissioned by Christ to bring the gospel to the world. After Pentecost, the Spirit became Christ's missionary presence in the world (Matt. 28:16–20; Luke 24:48–49). He lives in each believer as the Spirit of witness (Acts 1:8). John says succinctly, "And the Spirit is the witness because the Spirit is the truth" (1 John 5:7 RSV). He is uniquely committed to witnessing to the power and reality of Jesus' blood sacrifice, as we see in 1 John 5:8: "There are three witnesses, the Spirit, the water, and the blood; and these three agree" (RSV). The Spirit has one supreme concern: to testify to the washing away of sins by a bloody, substitutionary atonement. It could not be otherwise than that we who have the Spirit living within us should share in His missionary calling.

Communicating this understanding of the Holy Spirit's filling can transform attitudes on evangelizing in the local church. Tom's fears are common to many of us, both leaders and followers. He properly sensed that he, as an individual believer, must witness, but he had not seen his personal testimony as part of the work of the ongoing kingdom of Christ. He had failed to see that his witness was not meant to be carried out in his own strength, but rather with the believing boldness that comes from the Holy Spirit.

The Holy Spirit imparts the gift of boldness (παρρεσια and πληροφορια) to the believer as he prays (Acts 1:13–14; 2:1; 2:42; 3:1; 4:13–31; Eph. 6:18–20).[1] The new Christian receives courage to witness as a fulfillment of his new identity (Luke 24:49), enabling him to share Christ while forgetting about his own reputation and safety (Acts 1:8; 4:13–31).

This boldness is characterized by three qualities: contrition, certainty, and confrontation. A "bold" witness that lacks these characteristics may simply be aggressive or presumptuous, with words issuing from the flesh, not the Spirit. However, the Christian who asks the Holy Spirit for biblical boldness may be assured not only of growing freedom from his own fear, but of the conversion of many souls, since his witness will bear the marks of divine reality. Let's examine the first of these characteristics.

<u>*Contrition,*</u> or sorrow for sin, might seem to have little to do with boldness in witness, but Scripture indicates that those who witnessed with Spirit-empowered boldness first experienced a deep conviction and sorrow over sin. Peter's bitter tears of repentance preceded his vibrant transformation (Matt. 26:75). The believers of the Jerusalem church had been "pierced to the heart" by their sin (Acts 2:37; 4:31). And the Apostle Paul describes himself as "the chief of sinners" and a "wretched man" (1 Tim. 1:15; Rom. 7:24).

This brokenness over sin is inherent in the new work which the Holy Spirit initiated at the cross (Luke 23:48; John 19:37) and climaxed in Peter's preaching at Pentecost (Acts 2:37). Such unusual mourning had been prophesied by Zechariah in his prophetic vision of the outpouring of the Spirit at Pentecost. Here, the beholding of a pierced God and mourning of the deepest kind are inseparable (Zech. 12:10–14).

Some professing Christians may fear that an emphasis on repentance morbidly accentuates sin and furthers psychological self-despising. Certainly the Scriptures portray a sorrow unto death in the experiences of King Saul, Esau, and Judas. But a godly sorrow for sin such as came with power at Pentecost moves in another direction. This sorrow is healing and liberating, effecting a cleansing of the deepest fountains of life. Repentance in this case is simply coming to understand and experience the cross from God's point of view. It is seeing that the breaking of the Lord reveals a righteous God's assessment of our guilt and corruption. Such a conviction frees us for witness by squashing self-righteousness and reminding us again of what God in love has done to save sinners.

<u>Biblical repentance</u> is a sorrow that becomes the <u>doorway</u> to full assurance of forgiveness, devotion to Christ and one another, and a life of praise, prayer, and gentle but fearless witness. When we come to understand the Father's love for us in the face of our rebellion and sin, the Holy Spirit gives us the boldness to love, without fear, others who are as needy as we.

The prophet Isaiah experienced this progression as an Old Testament saint. His first response at seeing the Lord in His fiery majesty and holiness was a deep conviction of his own sin, but it was followed quickly by a burden for his neighbors—"I dwell in the midst of a people of unclean lips" (Isa. 6:5). Isaiah's humbling before the Lord freed him from fear and filled him with love for the people who needed his message.

A second characteristic of biblical boldness is *certainty*. Even on a human level, people are not persuaded by a testimony filled with doubts and questions. The need for authority and assurance applies even more to issues of faith. We cannot persuade others to accept a message that we ourselves only half believe. Boldness in witness must spring from a certainty of faith which God gives to the humble and contrite (Isa. 6:1–8). We can witness effectively only to that which we have learned firsthand in our brokenness before God (John 3:11; 4:29).

The Spirit is eager to supply us with unshakable assurance. As sons of God, we are entitled to complete certainty of Christ's living reality as the Lord of glory (John 20:31). We can claim it for two reasons: the certainty of the Spirit's authenticating presence and the certainty of the facts given through apostolic testimony. Both elements are expressed clearly in Jesus' statement to the disciples: "But when the Helper comes, whom I will send to you from the Father, He will bear witness of me, and you will bear witness also, because you have been with me from the beginning" (John 15:26–27 NASB). The Spirit of truth kept the disciples faithful to the facts in reporting what they had seen, and at Pentecost indwelt them as the Spirit of truth and witness. Hence the Spirit as the primary witness to Christ's work acts through the testimony of the apostles, whose message He has preserved in the flawless Scriptures.

The infallibility of our message should lead to great confidence in our witness. Why then do so many Bible-believing Christians seem to lack it? They appear to believe all the right things about the Scriptures, yet I fear that, for many, the assent is simply mental. Christ is not a compelling reality in their lives. No wonder they hesitate to witness! We need to search our hearts for pharisaism, for the sin of studying the Word as an end in itself for purely intellectual purposes (John 5:37–47). We want to escape Jesus' severe condemnation: "You do not have His word abiding in you" (John 5:38 RSV).

The antidote for such a powerless orthodoxy is to see by faith that Scripture is intended to lead us to God Himself through a living, reigning Jesus Christ who is coming again. The Scriptures preach to us a living, risen Lord. And grounded in that firsthand knowledge of Christ, our testimony can convince men of the reality of our living Lord Jesus.

I vividly recall an experience I had as a youthful unbeliever, steeped in intellectual despising of the Christian faith. It was August 1945, and the atomic bomb had just been exploded over Hiroshima. As we commuters boarded our bus, people were shaking their heads and wondering whether this new weapon would destroy the world. A sailor responded quietly, "No, the world won't ever be destroyed by atomic bombs. Jesus won't let that happen. He's coming back first." As an unbeliever, I was completely silenced by this weapon of unquestioning confidence. It was biblical boldness, grounded on a certainty that came from the Spirit of God, that defeated my unbelief.

Loving *confrontation*, the third aspect of biblical boldness, flows from our certainty of Christ's sovereignty in the universe. Because we know for sure that the cross has given way to a crown, we are willing, indeed compelled, to confront men with the message of the gospel. We do this because we believe that the King's rights require submission to His living lordship. "The evangelization of the world," wrote John R. Mott, "is not man's enterprise but God's. Christ at the right hand of God is the leader of the missionary movement, and with him resides all power in heaven and on earth. . . . Faith is the victory that overcomes the world."[2]

Such a confrontation requires a clear statement of the message. A person cannot be confronted with Christ's redemptive rule until he sees its nature clearly and understands that it *requires* his conversion. Paul had this in mind when, in Ephesians 6:20, he asked for prayer that he might preach *"boldly, as I ought* to speak." In the parallel passage in Colossians 4:4, he makes the same request by asking "that I may make it *clear* in the way I ought to speak" (NASB). "Clear" and "bold" are virtually interchangeable terms here, and they remind us that confrontation is not a psychological domination or entrapment, but a presentation of truth that brings a person face to face with Christ.

Read the messages recorded by Luke in Acts. All of them are clear, specific, and confrontational in character. They touch men at their most vulnerable points. On the day of Pentecost, Peter bluntly rebukes his hearers as the murderers of the Son of God (Acts 2:22–23, 36). In Athens, Paul does not talk about the sins of the Jews but about the idolatry of the Greeks (Acts 17:22–24).

Such confrontation does not mean that we ignore good manners or that we force truth on people who are not ready to receive it. We must be quick to respect human dignity and deal with questions in patient humility. But we also take it as a God-given norm that the work of evangelism requires, as one evangelist has said, standing "directly before the heart's door of a sinner and clearly confront[ing] him with the Gospel of Christ."[3]

One older teenager in our congregation does this by picking up hitchhikers and greeting them in the following friendly way: "Hello, I'm Richard Doe, and I want to share with you that Christ is alive." The quality of the ensuing conversations is usually excellent, and hitchhikers confronted in this way rarely give trouble.

Another member, a truck driver, visits hospitals. He often opens a conversation like this: "My reason for visiting you is to let you know about the love of Jesus, that there is nothing better in the whole world than knowing Him." In one instance, five members of a family were brought to Christ through reading a Bible left with a dying young man.

We are also blessed with two young women who visit nearby college campuses. Their approach has been simply to introduce themselves to students and ask, "May we have a few minutes of your time to talk to you about Jesus Christ and the new life He gives?" A number of students have been converted through their ministry.

What we seek, in short, is to get enough truth before men in a personal, loving manner that they may see their responsibility to act before the hour of opportunity has passed. The sovereign King is coming. Therefore, a witness empowered by biblical boldness must be clear, compassionate, confrontational, and confident: confident that the Holy Spirit who inspired the testimony will also apply it to the hearts of those who hear. The Spirit is God's ultimate weapon (Joel 2:28–32; Luke 3:16; John 16:7–11).

Finding the Cutting Edge

1. What are the three marks of biblical boldness?
2. Think of the human idea of a "bold person." What does this concept include? How does that differ from biblical boldness? What in biblical boldness is not found in the non-Christian view of courage?
3. What is the connection between a humble contrition and the certainty of faith? Between certainty and confrontation?
4. How does biblical contrition differ from a morbid concentration on your sins? See Psalms 34:18; 51:10–17; Luke 18:9, 14; 2 Corinthians 7:9–10; James 4:1–10.
5. List the steps necessary for you to have biblical boldness in your life and witness. Begin with your fears (2 Tim. 1:6–12); include the role of the Holy Spirit (Luke 12:11), the power of promise-centered prayer (Luke 11:13), and courage in witness (Acts 1:8–14).
6. The cutting edge of grace: Draw up an action plan for increasing your boldness in witness based upon the steps listed in 5 above.

Notes

1. Cf. Heinrich Schlier, TDNT, 5: "Παρρεσια, freedom towards God, the right and power to say anything to God, is to be found where a man, taught by the Spirit to obey the commandments of Jesus, and at one with the will of God, opens his heart to God in prayer" (p. 881). He adds, "It also includes openness in the gospel. . . . Above all the discussion in II Cor. 3:12ff. shows

that for Paul παρρεσια to God—the uncovered face of Paul looking towards Him, 3:18—implies an uncovered face which men can see as Israel could not see the covered face of Moses, 3:13. He who lifts up his face uncovered to God also turns uncovered to men" (p. 883).

2. John R. Mott, *The Evangelization of the World in This Generation* (New York: Arno Press, 1972), 129–30.

3. C. E. Autrey, *Basic Evangelism* (Grand Rapids: Zondervan, 1959), 27.

The Father can bestow no higher
or more wonderful gift than this: His
own Holy Spirit, the Spirit of sonship.
This truth naturally suggests the
thought that this first and chief gift
of God must be the first and chief
object of all prayer. For every need of
the spiritual life this is the one thing
needful: the Holy Spirit. . . . If we but
yield ourselves entirely to the disposal
of the Spirit, and let Him have His way
with us, He will manifest the life of
Christ within us.

—ANDREW MURRAY,
WITH CHRIST
IN THE SCHOOL OF PRAYER

FIVE

Prayer and the Promises: Power Source for Bold Ministry

LET'S NOW FACE A PAINFUL BUT HELPFUL TRUTH: the boldness of grace cannot come from our natural selves. I am naturally (that is, in my sinful nature inherited from my first parents) self-contained and self-praising. I tend to seek assurance of my righteousness by comparing myself with others—judging them as sinners and myself as more or less sin-free (Luke 18:9–14). Following the example of a friend, I must identify myself this way: "My name is Jack Miller, and I am a recovering Pharisee."

If you read the parable of the Pharisee and the tax collector in Luke 18, you might conclude that I speak too severely about myself. I am not usually a strict, rigid, unfeeling religious person as is the man in the parable. But there is still enough of the Pharisee in me—and, I believe, in every one of us. The Pharisee is essentially a person who is more aware of the sins of others than of his own; he consequently feels superior to other human beings and judges them without first taking the beam out of his own eye (Luke 6:39ff.). He also lacks loving hope. He does not expect grace to do much for him or others.

We recovering Pharisees often find that in our minds we have collected albums full of dark snapshots of other people, ourselves, and God and His grace. What is real in our minds are negative images of the resistance of non-Christians to the gospel, our own failed attempts at witnessing, and feelings of powerful self-condemnation at work beneath our proclaimed righteousness.

But here our need makes us teachable. Grace, not sin, is the governing power in our lives, and therefore it stirs us to look at the way prayer and the promises can become the power source for bold ministry. We begin by looking more closely at the teaching about prayer in the Gospel of Luke and Acts.

The book of Acts makes it plain that the bold witness described in the previous chapters is God's norm for His church. After Pentecost, we see that Peter and John are characterized by incredible courage in proclaiming the good news (Acts 4:13), and they do not stand alone. Stephen's fearlessness in witness and debate surpasses even the boldness of the apostles (Acts 6–7). The same fervent tongue is also found in the church as a whole. Believers are not silenced by persecution. Instead, those "who were scattered went about preaching the Word" (Acts 8:4 RSV).

How did this happen? In the Old Testament, God's bold ones were few in number. How, suddenly, did the whole church of God begin to function like God's special prophets of old? The answer lies in the coming of the Holy Spirit, the Spirit of witness who, as He indwells men and women, enlists and equips them to do His work. The Father sends the Spirit because the Son has atoned for our sins. At the institution of the new covenant Jesus says, "This is my blood of the new covenant that is poured out for many for the forgiveness of sins" (Matt. 26:28). Linked to this covenant of pardon and acceptance is the gift of the Spirit who works faith and adoption in those who once were enemies of grace. The inseparable order now is justification by faith in Christ's atonement, adoption to sonship, and the gift of the Spirit (Gal. 3:10–14; 4:4–7).

There is something else too. God provides a means for us to appropriate the Spirit's power in our lives and a means for non-Christians to be prepared to receive the Word. That means is prayer. It breaks down our self-sufficiency. It is our door of access to the Heavenly Father through which, as His adopted sons and daughters, we receive His grace to do His work. Again, it is the Holy Spirit who brings our prayers to the Father. These prayers often come with weakness and feeble groanings. But they have compelling authority because they are offered in the name of the omnipotent Son of God and carried by the intercession of the Spirit of adoption.

The coming of the Holy Spirit and the believer's consequent new access and power in prayer are what make the difference between the Old Testament church and New Testament church. Under the old covenant, God's people were notorious for not stirring themselves up to pray (Isa. 64:7). But Christ's resurrection and ascension ushered in a new age when His people were indwelt by the Spirit of prayer. This Spirit warms our hearts to approach the Father and makes intercession for us so that our prayers may be heard. The church pictured by Luke is first and foremost a confident, expectant church because it is a dependent, praying church. These Christians had been shown the vital link between prayer for grace and the work God gave them to do. They knew:

- that the Lord taught His disciples to seek the gift of the Spirit through earnest prayer (Luke 11:1–13);
- that the Lord commanded His disciples to wait together in Jerusalem until they were filled with the power of the Spirit (Luke 24:49);
- that His disciples obeyed the Lord by waiting with "one mind" in constant and united prayer for the coming of the Holy Spirit (Acts 1:13–24; 2:1–4);
- that the disciples were filled with the Spirit of grace while they prayed at Pentecost (Acts 2:1–4), and subsequently when they sought power to confront a hostile world with renewed boldness (Acts 4:22–31);
- that the apostles were unalterably committed to prayer as their first priority in ministry (Acts 6:4);
- and that one of the four distinguishing features of their newly born church was its being devoted continually to the practice of public prayer (Acts 2:42).[1]

In short, what the church of Jerusalem had discovered was that the work of the gospel required the gift of the Spirit's filling, sought in fervent prayer. Here is an amazing paradox: we who *have* the Holy Spirit must constantly *seek* His presence and His control of our lives by fervent prayer (Luke 11:5–13). Without this heavenly anointing, there is only an earthly work. Our words have no power unless the Spirit speaks through us, and they have no effect unless the Spirit applies them to men's hearts. John Piper says, "God has made the spread of his fame hang on the preaching of his Word; and he has made the preaching of his Word hang on the prayers of the saints."[2]

It is sad today that many believers who are sensitive to doctrinal issues are often insensitive to the vital link between evangelism and prayer. They emphasize the power of the written Word, but have less awareness of the necessity for united and continued prayer that God would powerfully apply that Word to sinners through the Spirit. Commonly, these orthodox Christians have a certain fear of fervent public prayer among believers. Not only are they afraid of displays of "enthusiasm," but they feel that the main task of the church at this end time is to hold the line, to maintain true doctrine, and to wait for God—rather than petition Him—to accomplish His sovereign good pleasure in the area of evangelism.

These believers are perfectly right in their determination to defend the faith in our time. Perhaps that is why it is difficult for them to see that they may be heretical when it comes to the doctrine of prayer. But it is a most serious deviation in doctrine to neglect the teaching that all Christian work hinges on the supplication of God's people and "the supply of the Spirit of Jesus Christ" (Phil. 1:19).

Then there are other believers who are sensitive to the importance of prayer, but who tend to think of it almost as a commodity, a vehicle for carrying forward the next evangelistic campaign. These zealous Christians are so intensely concerned with enlisting "prayer support" for the work that they stand in danger of equating prayer support with other kinds of support—material means and organizational structures.

Again, these believers are perfectly right in their recognition of the necessity of prayer. But this proper emphasis may well mislead them into thinking that they need no further instruction on the wonder of our access to the living God through Christ. As a result, they are robbed of the blessing of further growth in the doctrine of prayer and miss seeing the magnificence of God's glory as the supreme purpose of it all. They also may unwittingly fall into the grave error of attempting to manipulate God as did Israel in the days of Eli (1 Sam. 4).

Christians in both situations have missed the exciting link between prayer and God's purposes in the world. It is, simply, that *prayer starts the promises of God on their way to fulfillment.* Here is God's battle plan for our time. In prayer, God allows us to lay hold of His purposes as these are expressed in His promises. Each promise is a hook for pulling our faith into the heavens. There we catch God's missionary vision of a world filled with His praise (Ps. 67). By claiming God's promises as we petition Him in prayer, we set God's work in motion (Luke 10:1–3; Acts 4:23–31). Unbelievable as it may seem, the omnipotent God uses our requests to activate the fulfillment of His mighty promises in history (Rev. 8:1–5). As the laborers pray, He begins to ripen the harvest for reaping (Acts 13:1–4).

As a leader in the colonial church, Jonathan Edwards understood this principle better than most. In the late 1740s he reasoned in an essay entitled "An Humble Attempt to Promote Explicit Agreement in Prayer" that revival and missionary outthrust inevitably resulted when believers committed themselves, unitedly and continuously, to intercession for this purpose.[3] As an example, he cited the revival through prayer of the Cambuslang Presbytery in Scotland. In his view, this and other mighty outpourings of the Spirit did not happen by caprice, but came about because of the inherent connection between prayer and the descent of the Spirit. In essence, he taught that a concert of prayer to claim the biblical promises resulted in the fulfillment of great passages like Zechariah 8:20–23. There verses 21 and 22 picture a great concert of prayer by God's people, and verse 23 reveals the result, when many men from the nations take "hold of the skirt of the Jew" and commit themselves to the living God.

According to historians of revival, Edwards's teaching on the power of agreement in prayer stimulated a whole series of revivals and conversions throughout the 1700s. By the close of the century, American Christians came to understand that coldness and timidity in evangelism in the church could only be cured by a commitment to corporate prayer. According to J. Edwin Orr, a major student of revivals, this "concert of prayer" became the dynamic source of boldness in evangelism and missionary endeavor for the U.S. right up to the mighty spiritual explosion of 1858. He says, "The concert of prayer remained the significant factor in the recurring revivals of religion and the extraordinary out-thrust of missions for a full fifty years, so commonplace it was taken for granted by the Churches."[4]

Bold praying has its impact on the individual as well. We have seen that such intercession brings the harvest to fruition by claiming the promises of God; it also becomes the power that activates the laborers. The reason for this is that boldness in witness is fed by boldness in worship and intercession. Left to ourselves, we Christians are not in the habit of witnessing. Our habitual relationships with friends, relatives, and co-workers are ones of conventional reserve. But, when we have spoken first with God and claimed the promise of the Spirit's power and presence, we cannot be silent before men.

The important thing is to *begin* to pray for the salvation of particular people no matter how one feels, and thereafter to *keep on* praying whether visible results appear or not. Find a Christian friend or two, share the biblical vision of the harvest with them, and gather together weekly to pray with one mind for the Spirit to convict non-Christians of sin, break down their prejudices and fears, and open their hearts to Christ.

Prayer with this kind of boldness and power depends upon our understanding of Christ's work for us. We can pray this way only when we understand that the blood of Jesus has given us free access to the Father. Listen to Hebrews.

> Since therefore, brethren, we have confidence [boldness] to enter the holy place by the blood of Jesus, by a new and living way which He inaugurated for us through the veil, that is, His flesh, and since we have a great high

priest over the house of God, let us draw near with a sincere heart in full assurance of faith, having our hearts sprinkled clean from an evil conscience and our bodies washed with pure water. (10:19–22 NASB)

Jesus' work introduced a new day in God's relationship with man. The veil of the old covenant between a holy God and unholy men has been forever removed by the sacrifice of Christ. Now there is nothing between. Friendship, openness, access, and freedom describe the new relationship between the Father and those who know Him through His Son. Hence boldness in worship is nothing but the sons of God exercising their new rights through the power of the Spirit.

These new rights, however, cannot be exercised in the absence of a clear conscience. We must not hide anything from our Father or pretend that we are without sin (1 John 1:5–2:2). We are not orphans, slaves of fear, who love the secrets of darkness. No, we are the beloved sons and daughters of a gracious Father. We believe His promise and confess our sins freely to Him. By faith we draw near to Him, "having our hearts sprinkled clean from an evil conscience" (Heb. 10:22 NASB). The tense of the verb in the Greek implies a past action extending into the present in its effect. This is what Jesus' blood has done for us. His past action has accomplished our permanent acceptance as sons with the Father. It also provides for a continued cleansing of the conscience through the daily confession of sins on the basis of that finished work.

This is how we learn to enjoy the full freedom Christ has purchased for us, and it is the only way a Spirit-empowered evangelism can proceed unhindered by barriers of selfishness, unrepented sin, and a guilty conscience. When the Spirit worked powerfully in Isaiah's life to make him a man of courage, it began with the man's immediate confession of a particular sin, a sin of the lips. He had become honest about himself for the first time, and in a most public way. It is this kind of repentance that prepares the way for bold prayers of faith and a bold witness fulfilling those prayers.

How would this freedom express itself in the local church or on a missions team? My guess is that it often comes with a divine surprise, with people doing what is not really natural for them to do.

For instance, some years ago Richard Kaufmann, now a pastor but then an elder in our New Life Presbyterian Church, gave himself to bold praying for the salvation of his neighbors. He urged the rest of us leaders to pray with him, and we did, claiming the promises together. His burden kept growing for his neighbors' salvation, and I expected him to invite them to a Bible study in his home. Instead, with the agreement of his hospitable wife Elizabeth, he went to them and apologized for not being more neighborly! They accepted his apology and some said they regretted that they had not been very neighborly themselves.

Then he did neighborly things. He went out of his way to greet them and talk with them. Finally he invited them to an open house, and the first time he and his family did that, over forty people showed up. Within a few more weeks, professions of faith followed, and one of these neighbors is now a deacon in the church.

Finding the Cutting Edge

1. Name the six links between prayer and the work God gives us to do.
2. Evaluate your own practical theology of prayer. Check the statements that most accurately describe your view and practice.
___ I don't pray much. God is sovereign and I trust Him to run the world without being dependent upon my prayers.
___ God is my good Father and I pray to Him for grace to witness.
___ I pray a great deal, but it does not seem to work for me. God seems indifferent to my prayers. I'm disappointed in Him.
___ I pray for a parking place downtown and always find one.

_____ I mostly pray for the sick.

_____ I especially pray when I am afraid. I don't know much about praise.

_____ Praying with others is hard for me, so I stay away from prayer gatherings.

_____ Praying with others is hard for me, so I go as often as I can to prayer gatherings.

_____ I study the promises of God so that I can pray for small things and also for God to convict people of sin and bring them to Jesus.

3. State in one sentence the connection between prayer and the promises of God. Then claim a prayer promise like John 15:7–8.

4. Write a paragraph on Jonathan Edwards's work promoting corporate prayer and bold evangelism.

5. A troubled conscience is a hindrance to effective evangelism. How does our sonship relationship enable us to be freed from crippling guilt?

6. The cutting edge of grace: On a three-by-five card write (at the top) a promise or invitation to faith, such as John 3:16 or 1:29 or 15:7–8. Underneath that promise list the names of five people you want to see become Christians. Then put the card on a mirror where you will see it at least once a day. Each time you see the card, claim its promise for the five persons.

Notes

1. Cf. Harvie M. Conn, "Luke's Theology of Prayer," *Christianity Today* 17 (December 22, 1972), 6–8. I also wish to acknowledge Professor Conn's lectures on prayer given at Westminster Theological Seminary as contributing to these insights.

2. John Piper, *The Pleasures of God: Meditations on God's Delight in Being God* (Portland, Ore.: Multnomah, 1991), 231.

3. Jonathan Edwards, "An Humble Attempt to Promote Explicit Agreement and Visible Union of God's People, in Extraordinary Prayer, for the Revival of Religion and the Advancement of Christ's Kingdom on Earth," *Works* (Worcester: Isaiah Thomas, Jr., 1808), 3:355–494.

4. J. Edwin Orr, *The Fervent Prayer: The Worldwide Impact of the Great Awakening of 1858* (Chicago: Moody Press, 1974), xi.

*B*ut God's intentions aren't just personal; they are corporate as well. From the beginning, our God has longed to create for Himself a community that would reign with Him forever. He plans [and He has already begun] to bring into being a new international community of reconciliation, peace, and celebration. . . .We will be one in Christ, worshipping our God as one gigantic family.

—TOM SINE,
WHY SETTLE FOR MORE
AND MISS THE BEST?

Six

The Community of Joy: The Special Power of a Corporate Witness

ONE OF THE MOST ASTONISHING ASPECTS of the birth of the church in Jerusalem goes virtually unmentioned by its historian, Luke. Consider the vitality of this newly born congregation: it attracts more permanent disciples in several weeks than did Jesus in three concentrated years of ministry in Judea and Galilee! How amazing that feeble human beings should see more fruit than the Lord Himself while He was on earth! Yet it is clear that this was God's intention. Holy "fear came upon every soul" that encountered the church in those days (Acts 2:43). By God's hand, men were daily compelled to faith by the supernatural quality of the church community (Acts 2:47). Christ was risen. That was the unshakable fact of history. Naturally, everybody who believed this fact was filled with incredible joy.

What we see here is the fulfillment of Jesus' promise that those who believed in Him should accomplish greater works than He did during the days of His earthly ministry (John 14:12). And it is clear from Luke's account that the Holy Spirit used the *community* of believers, Christ's body, to perform that multiplication of Christ's work. Their witness together was powerful in the hands of the Holy Spirit. It was powerful because they had become the community of the forgiven, the forgiven who knew they were utterly unworthy of being forgiven and who now responded with deep humility and inexpressible gladness to the grace received.

We have seen in the past few chapters the way in which the Holy Spirit applies the gospel message to make individual believers bold in worship and witness. What Luke has recorded in Acts shows us that He does the same thing for Christ's people *as a body*. As the Spirit leads us into a deeper understanding of Christ's work on our behalf, our life as a witnessing community becomes a formidable testimony to the power of God.

Paul supplies a striking illustration of the way this happens in his first letter to the Corinthians. Concerning a church service even in that backslidden congregation, Paul could write, "But if all prophesy, and an unbeliever or an ungifted man enters, he is convicted by all, he is called to account by all; the secrets of his heart are disclosed; and so he will fall on his face and worship God, declaring that God is certainly among you" (1 Cor. 14:24–25 NASB). Paul simply assumes that any normal worship service will lay bare the hearts of the unconverted and cause them to repent before the living God.

How could Paul have such confidence? The answer can only be that he understood the Holy Spirit's purpose in planting the church in the world. The church in its richness of gifts and graces is Christ's sole missionary representative among men. In its corporate life and rich diversity of gifts working by love, it is the image of Christ to the world, God's ambassador by which He makes Himself known to man. That is why in another astonishing passage, the apostle actually calls the church of God "Christ." In 1 Corinthians 12:12, he says, "For as the body is one and has many members, but all the members of that one body, being many, are one body, so also is Christ" (NKJV). Logically, what you would expect as the climax of Paul's analogy between the unity and diversity of the human body and the nature of the church would be: "So also is the church." Instead, Paul gives the church the most sacred name of all. To be sure, he is not teaching that the church is Christ's actual continuing incarnation. But he daringly emphasizes that the fullness of gifts in the body derives all its reality from Christ, and that it is His personality shining through the body of believers into the world. Thus it is fitting that the church be named after the source of its holy light.

If we accept the Christological nature of our corporate life, those of us who lead must modify the way we train believers to think of witnessing. I have in view the image of evangelism as fishing for the lost. Too often we have only stressed the single fisherman with his pole. There is certainly a place for him, but there is a danger that the "lone angler" concept will place undue emphasis on witnessing skills, techniques, and special gifts, discouraging Christians who lack these distinctive features. It is clear that for the church in Acts, evangelism was something that involved everyone—and they were often involved together. We need to focus on the biblical metaphor of fishermen pulling together as a team on the same net. Our shared life as the company of Christ's redeemed is at the very center of our gathering in of the lost.

This principle came to life for me in a rural pastorate I served some years ago. The church had had a history of conflicts widely known in the community and had a clouded reputation. But many in the church were sick of the strife and responded to the Spirit under the preaching of the gospel. As a body they began to look and act more like Christ. Gossip died down. The gifts of the Spirit began to flourish. The deacons faithfully sent flowers to any hospitalized sick in the community. Hot meals were taken to chronically ill persons. A spirit of prayer and intercession began to come in the prayer meetings. Visitors were impressed by a new attentiveness in the Sunday worship services. One of them remarked, "Before, when I visited, everybody read their bulletins or just looked around. But now they listen like hungry people. The change is so mysterious, it's frightening."

Good things replaced bad when people talked about the church, and as a consequence, within a few months the size of the congregation had nearly doubled. I realized that the Lord had permitted me to see a major principle of Christian leadership: to get out of the way and direct all the attention to what Christ has done for us in the gospel and to what He is now doing to beautify us in His own image. In this context, witnessing is fundamentally "gossiping" about the glory of the cross and its imprint on the life of Christ's people.

The church today faces two main problems when it comes to our corporate witness. The first is the hampering of our missionary oneness by our highly individualistic lives. Our thinking is so often self-centered that our oneness and mutual love in the Spirit is suppressed. We lose the vital unity and deep caring which belong to us because of our shared union with Christ. A congregation living according to what God says is normal, and reflecting Christ's love by the Spirit's power, would unfortunately strike most of us as exceptional—and maybe a little bit strange!

The second problem is an extreme in the other direction. It is the kind of corporate identity which conceals the power of Christ. It is a corporateness which is closed, exclusionary, and mechanically ritualistic. If you belong to the group, you are an "insider"; if you do not, you're an "outsider." There may be a measure of outward warmth in welcoming strangers, but basically the congregation is a closed tribe which demands a social change as well as a conversion of anyone who wishes to join. One can hardly be accepted as a full member of this kind of body without learning a specialized religious vocabulary embracing a narrow sectarian mind-set, and sometimes even adopting a particular style of dress.

Happily, the Christian pastor need not despair if he sees his congregation victimized by these errors. The Scripture is on your side, and God's sword is readily available to cut away both of these destructive tendencies. The Apostle Peter deals forcefully with both errors when he sets forth the biblical basis for a community witness and identity. He writes, "You are an elect race, a royal priesthood, a holy nation, a people for God's own possession, *in order that* you may shine forth the excellencies of Him who called you out of darkness into His marvelous light" (1 Peter 2:9). Here the apostle exposes a selfish individualism. Four times he gives us names which call attention to our being one people and not self-serving loners. We are in our origin, a race chosen of God, not just single worshipers; in our sanctity, one nation separated by God from the world, not just single citizens of the kingdom; and in our being, common property owned by God, not just single members of His body.

Furthermore, the subordinate conjunction translated "in order that" makes very clear that we do not exist for ourselves, as a local congregation or a particular denomination.[1] Our purpose, our reason for being, is to "shine forth the excellencies of Him who called us out of darkness into His marvelous light." We have been redeemed from the self-exalting and self-serving spirit of tribalism. Our very existence in the world involves our shining into the world's darkness. Tribalism makes everything center on preserving the status quo. It even perverts care for one another into a clannish self-love. But Peter confronts our selfishness with God's great "in order that." As God's "new people," we are present among men *in order that* we together may represent Christ to them through our united praise of God. I believe that there are four key ways in which our corporate witness can demonstrate the transforming power of Christ.

Our United Testimony

Our verbal testimony to the truth of the gospel is grounded in our conscious identification of ourselves as the people of God. We are called to affirm that we are united in our identity as the people Christ redeemed from the spiritually nameless of the earth. Together we await our glorious inheritance in our coming King (1 Peter 1:3–9).

This united witness to Christ's present lordship and imminent return has more than psychological value for the believer. It also carries special weight in establishing the truth of the gospel before a doubting world. Scripture states that truth is established by the testimony of those who know and have seen. Such a testimony requires corporate validation; a single reporter is not enough. It was for that reason that the Lord chose a college of twelve to testify to the reality of His bodily resurrection. Later, He called the whole church to give united testimony to the transforming power of His resurrection. The churches that grow most rapidly today are the ones that understand their mission. As they are gripped by a joyous certainty about Christ's bodily resurrection and His coming again, they offer convincing testimony to unbelievers around them. The subsequent conversions have much to do with the church's stand *together as a community of faith.*[2]

A striking example of the power of a united testimony is found in John Wesley's shipboard encounter with a group of Moravians on his way to America to do "mission work." A terrific storm scared Wesley half to death while the fearless Moravians functioned together as a praising church. They prayed, sang, and preached the gospel with joy, but he was paralyzed with fear. It was this meeting with a community of faith that led to his realization that he was without the faith of a son of God. Subsequently he came to a sure reliance on Christ for justification while listening to the reading of Luther's commentary on Romans.

Our Worship

Our corporate worship is another way in which Christ's reality and power are demonstrated to the world. Wherever the gospel is preached in the power of the Spirit, life-transforming effects inevitably follow (1 Thess. 1:5–10). As believers in assembly hear the gospel of Christ, they are led to adore Him. By faith they confess their sins to God and to one another (Prov. 28:13; 1 John 1:8–10; James 5:16). To prevent hardness of heart they submit to mutual exhortation (Heb. 3:6–13). In addition to responding to the Word proclaimed by ordained officers, they use the Scriptures to teach one another with the wisdom distributed throughout the body by the Holy Spirit (Col. 3:16). In this body-life setting, God is so evidently at work that, as we noted before, the casual visitor is brought to conviction of sin and conversion as "the secrets of his heart are disclosed" (1 Cor. 1:24–25 NASB).

Furthermore, this gathering of God's people is no ordinary fellowship. Here God meets with His people in heavenly fellowship, angel hosts converge, and Satan and his allies flee as lives are renewed. The holy is here and it is all-conquering.

In such a setting we hardly need to command witnessing. We

only need to <u>channel the zeal stirred up by the Spirit.</u> Having said this, however, we must acknowledge that we cannot assume that every gathering of God's people will experience the fullness of His presence. Even a quick reading of Revelation 1–3 will show that it is all too easy to suppose that God is with us when He is not. Hence as leaders we must raise up constant prayer for every last one of our meetings, that they will be real meetings with God, resulting in changed lives. The whole point of the history of redemption is that when Immanuel is present, transforming deeds of love follow. Things human are turned upside down. When God is truly present in a worship service, we can be sure that the Word of God will be sanctifying believers and converting non-Christians.

But there is a cost to be paid if this kind of worship life is to prevail in congregations. A pastor especially needs a combination of wisdom and courage in his preaching ministry in order to foster love and joy in a community of faith. He must take into account (i.e., exercise wisdom) that his hearers vary widely in their responses to the gospel. Some have heard it and have had their lives changed by it. Others have heard it and understood it, but have never acted on it. And yet others have never heard it in a way that we could say they understand it.

In his sermons <u>the preacher must apply the gospel to all three groups and call those who have never been changed by it to repentance and faith.</u> This takes courage. An aged Christian Reformed pastor once put it like this: "If you preach as though all your hearers were converted, you are deceiving them and yourself. You must labor to bring Christ to them; only then will they have life."

Our Ministries of Mercy

The church's understanding of herself as "once . . . no people" who are "now the people of God" determines not only our actions *before* the world, but *with* unbelievers around us as well. Perhaps the most important way is our diaconal care of the poor. Through it, we act out by deeds of love the message of the gospel. For what is that message? It is that the Highest became the lowest to lift us up from the depths of sin into the riches of His royal palace. As recipients of the abundant mercy, we are compelled by our new-found wealth in Christ to share it verbally and practically in deeds of kindness to the widow, the orphan, the sick, and the poor. This is the emphasis of James 1 and 2, and the theme of Romans 15 and 2 Corinthians 8 and 9. It is also the story of church history. Be it the Reformation or the Great Awakening, history shows that revival expresses itself in a concern for the weak that brings many of them to Jesus Christ.

This ministry of mercy requires thought and preparation, as well as a willingness to serve those who may not be especially thankful and, on occasion, to be taken advantage of by deceivers. Prudence has its place, but excessive caution is crippling. In one church where I held a series of evangelistic meetings, I urged the deacons to become more aggressive in helping widows and the poor. They replied with embarrassed candor, "We have been trying to do this. But the woman who writes the checks for our diaconal fund always refuses to write any because she never thinks the people are really needy!" This dear lady had kept the deacons of her church from making mistakes by preventing them from showing mercy!

By contrast the deacons in a California Christian Reformed Church that I served for a time seemed ready for anything. Once a family of fruitpickers was stranded on the highway with a ruined car engine. A quick call to the chairman of the deacons produced a tow truck, with the disabled car on its way to a service station owned by another deacon. Soon the husband was putting in another engine paid for by the deacons, while his wife and their children were seated in a nearby park eating a meal supplied by the deacons. In such a setting it was natural to share the gospel with these grateful people.

Our Hospitality

Closely allied to our care of the poor is the use of hospitality to express our community witness to men. We are right to seek to care for the needy and bring them to Christ. But the needy don't want our material gifts dropped in their laps, so to speak, from a speeding car! Our material gifts and our gift of the gospel are accepted as we also offer ourselves to them in hospitality. Biblical hospitality has escaped the pretensions of social entertaining which seeks to present the hosts to their best advantage. Rather, it provides the occasion in which the hosts may share themselves as they are, in the simplicity of their dependence on Christ and in the profusion of love and gifts they have received from Him.[3]

There is no question that such hospitality is often difficult for middle-class Christians. It is why many Christian homes have never hosted unsaved guests. It is also why many evangelical churches have fled "changing neighborhoods" for the suburbs. The dispossessed of the earth are often the unwashed, and sometimes they are the destructive. Nevertheless, Scripture makes it clear that we cannot worry about our image in the neighborhood or the wear and tear on our furniture. We must go ahead and invite them, and trust the Holy Spirit to help us to love them.

The same principle applies to our response to visitors to our services. People of all kinds come when they have been truly welcomed. But Christ's welcome cannot have reservation. A smile in the sanctuary is not enough; we must be willing to welcome them into our homes too. In this domestic setting the common faith of God's people takes visible and natural expression. No matter what sort of evangelism your church undertakes—door-to-door, open-air, or special revival meeting —you will lose the people your efforts bring in if they are not fully welcomed with the dignity and love God intended the church to offer them.

THE FOUR AREAS SET FORTH in this chapter as basic to our corporate witness may seem elementary, even insignificant. Certainly they lack the drama of open-air evangelism and similar outreach efforts. But what is basic to all our evangelism is that God calls every believer to witness in and through the body of Christ in natural ways. The challenge facing the church—particularly its leaders—is to encourage a program concentrating on personal evangelism and at the same time developing the witness that the Holy Spirit has ordained for the church as a body. It is a big challenge, and satanic opposition is great. Many pastors have yet to preach the gospel plainly in their worship services. The formalism of church tradition has entombed many church meetings. Church buildings have become "consecrated" property that cannot be used for community outreach. Some denominations have replaced the primacy of gospel preaching with an emphasis on upholding abstract doctrine. Others have embraced the shallow "isms" of the liberal church—secularism, rationalism, and socialism—and have replaced the message of the cross with a social gospel that does not offend non-Christians.

Yet in all this, the gospel and the Spirit will be triumphant. God's purposes are such that the church will realize her purpose in the world, though some branches may be broken off in the blindness of their self-righteousness. The great fact that the church is Christ's missionary representative in the world cannot be displaced. We are His witnessing team in the world; we are His conquering army; we are His representatives inviting everyone to come to the party of grace. Nothing can stop us as we rely exclusively on His grace for witnessing power. The excellencies and deeds of God will shine into the world's darkness through our combined proclamation.

Finding the Cutting Edge

1. Complete the following: "Too often we have only stressed the single fisherman with his pole. There is certainly a place for him, but there is a danger that the 'lone angler' concept will place undue emphasis on witnessing skills. . . . We need to focus on the biblical metaphor of fishermen. . . ."
2. What four areas of church life are identified in this chapter as crucial for a congregation's "pulling together" in evangelism? What does each contribute to our corporate witness?

3. Find four people in your congregation and discuss these ideas with them individually. Be patient, give these insights time to "soak in," but keep talking with the four people. Probably you will want them to read this chapter.
4. The cutting edge of grace: Gather those interested into a discussion-and-prayer group to discover ways these ideas can be applied to your church and its outreach. Follow these four guidelines for your meetings:
   a. *The patience guideline.* Introduce new ideas gradually; do not force them upon people or feel rejected when people disagree or fail to understand.
   b. *The listening guideline.* Encourage others to talk; listen carefully to them. Do not gossip and do not permit others to do so.
   c. *The communication guideline.* Give plenty of illustrations and examples; give your own testimony, especially be willing to humble yourself by confessing your own faults.
   d. *The power guideline.* Always move the climax of the discussion on to prayer for the Spirit's presence based upon a promise.

Notes

1. Cf. Johannes Blauw, *The Missionary Nature of the Church: A Survey of the Biblical Theology of Mission* (South Pasadena, Calif.: William Carey Library, n.d.), 132.

2. Note Acts 2:32 and 1 John 1:1–5.

3. Two helpful popular guides for biblical hospitality are Karen Burton Mains's *Open Heart, Open Home* (Elgin, Ill.: David C. Cook, 1976) and Edith Schaeffer's *L'Abri* (Wheaton, Ill.: Tyndale House, 1969).

It is not enough to build your church and to stand in your pulpit and say, "Come." You have to go out and seek, if you would save. When the passion for souls dies out, then all sense of the reality of religion perishes. It is when we see Him healing men that we have faith in the great Physician; it is when we see the lost being saved that we believe in Christianity. When the passion for the lost dies out in the pulpit, men will shiver around its cold ashes instead of warming their souls at the blaze of a light which was kindled in the heavens.

—CHARLES L. GOODELL,
PASTOR AND EVANGELIST

SEVEN

The Pastor Models Personal Witness

THE PICTURE OF EVANGELISM we have sketched here—the transformed believer boldly sharing his faith, the church united in a powerful demonstration of the gospel at work—may be as much the source of dismay as encouragement to a pastor with an unresponsive church. The battle may appear lost before you begin. The fear, the apathy, the unbelief may be so great among the people you serve as pastor that the vision seems unattainable. You are hesitant to initiate even the most preliminary evangelistic efforts for fear that if they fail, any faint flicker of interest in witness would go out altogether.

But things need not go this way. Your efforts at evangelism can yield permanent habits of witness if you proceed along biblical lines. What are the biblical principles? The most important one is perhaps the simplest: learning by example—by *your* example! The central example for witness in the Scriptures is the church officer. The people are expected to imitate their leader (Phil. 3:17; 1 Thess. 1:6).

Note the pattern in the history of the New Testament church as set forth in Luke and Acts. First, the Great Commission is given to the Lord's disciples: "Repentance and forgiveness should be preached in his name to all nations, beginning at Jerusalem" (Luke 24:47 RSV).

Now consider how the apostles set the pattern after Pentecost. We saw in chapter 5 that they became models for witness by boldly preaching the gospel in Jerusalem (Acts 2–5). Stephen followed their pattern, preaching even more boldly than they (Acts 6–7). Apparently he perceived the new universal character of the church even before the apostles had seen it. As members of the Jerusalem congregation saw the example of apostolic boldness intensified in Stephen, they imitated their leaders when the church came under persecution (Acts 8:1, 4).

I do not believe that Luke's recording of these developments is casual. It is an integral part of the plan of the book of Acts which, in large part, is governed by Jesus' outline of the Great Commission in Acts 1:8: "And you shall be my witnesses in Jerusalem and in all Judea and in Samaria and to the end of the earth" (RSV). The scattering of the congregation into Judea and Samaria is the initiation of the second stage of the Lord's fulfillment of His own missionary mandate. And in carrying this work forward, the Spirit now uses not the apostles, but the people generally (along with evangelists such as Philip).

What the Spirit wants us to see is that the work of the Great Commission begins with the leaders, but it is also His good pleasure to have the whole congregation fulfill this ministry through the sovereignty of the Spirit. And in this early period of church history, let us note that the people soon appear to be more eager than the apostles to fulfill the terms of the Great Commission (Acts 8:1–4). They seem more soldierly, more earnest, about getting the gospel to everyone. They are the first ones to seek out the Gentiles without having the Gentiles initiate the encounter (Acts 11:19–24). In the setting of the contemporary local church, the parallel would be for the pastor and elders to begin evangelizing the middle class community only to have the rest of the congregation spontaneously reach out to black and Jewish neighbors as they caught the vision.

The same situation prevails later in Thessalonica. Into this European setting Paul and his missionary associates come and preach the gospel with great power and authority (1 Thess. 1:5).[1] Then the people, "having received the word in much tribulation, with the joy of the Holy Spirit," become imitators of the missionaries and the Lord (1 Thess. 1:6 NASB).

This imitation includes an amazing boldness in witness. "For," writes Paul, "the word of the Lord has sounded forth from you, not only in Macedonia and Achaia, but in every place your faith toward God has gone forth, so that we have no need to say anything" (1 Thess. 1:8 NASB).

What a remarkable situation! Paul has brought the gospel to the Thessalonians, and they function as an amplifier that re-broadcasts the gospel throughout the region of the eastern Mediterranean. Thus when Paul arrives in a new place, it seems that these Thessalonians have been there before him.

This recurrent pattern illustrating God's principles of evangelism also explains much about the contemporary evangelistic scene.

The first point: Ultimately, it is the Holy Spirit who fulfills the missionary mandate, but He has established a pattern for us to follow. The people evangelize when they have *been* evangelized. They also evangelize when they see their leaders evangelizing.

You who are pastors really have no reason to hope that your people will become zealous for evangelism any other way, for the example of church officers plays a crucial part in the biblical scheme. Not because they are intended to be the only ones witnessing (as often happens), but because it is their calling to equip the saints for the work of service (Eph. 4:12). Don't let your fear that your people will leave the evangelism to you deter you from a bold and visible witness before them. Lead them by your life and example, and patiently remind them that your work is intended as a *beginning* to a life of corporate witness in the church. This will require consistency, patience, love for your people, and a real burden for the lost on your part.

The second point: Sometimes people keep spreading the gospel when their leaders hold back the message through sluggishness or ignorance, but many stop evangelizing just because their leaders are not doing it. The church is filled to overflowing with examples of this sad chain reaction.

The third point: The Spirit of God lives in every member of

Christ's body (1 Cor. 12:13), and this Holy One is a witnessing, missionary spirit (John 15:26–27). For this reason evangelistic concern does not completely wither away in the congregation even though the office-bearers evidence little zeal for witness. But when the Spirit kindles a new flame of missionary life, that life may move *outside* the perimeter of the established church. It then comes to maturity without the wisdom of the larger body and the guidance of church leaders.

Ultimately these new forms of missionary life return to the established church as evangelistic organizations or even parachurch structures. When this happens, the pastors and elders may find themselves in the awkward position of opposing an evangelistic enterprise which, in spite of doctrinal deficiencies, is obviously being blessed by the Holy Spirit.

In all this there is a healthy jolt for pastors. Has the love of Christ constrained us to be missionary examples to our flocks? Or have we failed to evangelize in our preaching, in our own Sunday school, and in our neighborhood? Do our people breathe in from us a spirit of holy compassion for lost souls, or do they breathe in a spirit of ease in Zion and myopic indifference to the hell that awaits unsaved sinners?

Defining the Example

How can you as a pastor recover the New Testament model for witness? How can you begin to set an example for witness that the whole church will follow? Think for a moment of the biblical descriptions of the pastor to see what God would have you be.

You are a steward, having in your hands God's message and discipline, the keys to the kingdom. You are a herald and ambassador, bringing the good news of salvation from the King. You are an elder-bishop, an undershepherd, feeding and ruling over the flock in Christ's name, guided by the Word of God. You are also a teacher, expounding the Scriptures, exhorting, warning, and rebuking, all in relationship to sound doctrine in the Lord Jesus.

But be warned. If you think of yourself exclusively in those terms, you will very likely come across to men as a lord rather than as a helper for their joy (2 Cor. 1:24). In the New Testament the pastor is defined also as a *servant* and *brother* (John 13:1; 1 Cor. 1:1; 2 Cor. 1:2; Phil. 2:25). From Christ the elect servant and elder brother, the pastor learns to humble himself in love among the people as *their* servant and brother.

Try to teach and lead the people of God without this identification, and you will ring vaguely hollow to them. They will not readily follow you. But take a towel in your hand and wash their feet, and they will see Christ in you. Your example of Christ-like concern will be the model they need to become burdened themselves by the needs of others. Having received a measure of the love of Christ through you, they will be more able to extend it to those around them.

Suppose, for example, a Christian family is troubled by serious conflict between father and son. With patience and loving confrontation, you labor to bring them to shed old patterns of communication and put on Christian ways.

They are grateful and respond to the invitation to go witnessing with you. This emphasis on sharing Christ may sound premature since their problems are not fully resolved, but it has great therapeutic value because it begins to shift the emphasis away from themselves to Christ and His kingdom.

Thus, your evangelism will, as James Kennedy has taught us, be caught as well as taught.[2] Unfortunately, however, many pastors spend so little time with their people that the real man—and whatever concern he has for his sheep and the lost—is concealed behind a screen of distant professionalism. It certainly wasn't so with the Apostle Paul. Writing to the Thessalonian church, he notes that he was *gentle among them,* like a father and a nurse (1 Thess. 2:7, 11). He also mentions what he assumes they already know; he was not only ready to share the gospel with them, but also to give his life.

The remarkable thing is that nobody laughed. My guess is that if some of today's pastors stood before their congregations and made that announcement, smiling skepticism—at the very least—would be the response! How would your congregation react to such a declaration? Perhaps you are one who must admit that you give your people little to model themselves after. It is therefore not surprising that they lack the zeal and effectiveness of the Thessalonian church's evangelism—their pastor lacks the vision and fervor of the Apostle Paul.

The pastor functioning as a servant and brother knows that *work* is the operative word for his calling: the pastor is a *working* model for his people. Like Epaphroditus he may be called to labor in self-giving right to the door of death (Phil. 2:28–30), to study diligently as a scribe in the kingdom (Matt. 13:52; 2 Tim. 2:15), and to agonize in prayer for men (Col. 2:1–3; 4:12–13).

On a daily basis, this means that self-indulgence must be put to death in the pastor. Self-indulgence represents a special and continuing temptation to the pastor because his time is largely in his own hands. It takes the form of physical laziness and sluggishness of spirit, which readily fosters fear. Personal timidity and physical exhaustion often seem to issue from the poisoned conscience of the slothful leader.

It works like this: The pastor neglects his calling in the community, grows weary of study, and finds his preaching and teaching a burden. He also thinks he needs more sleep. And his fear of people grows.

Other sins soon spin out of his disobedient life. Legalistic penance, wheel-spinning, the aggressive pushing of secondary causes in the church, the neglect of matters of first importance— he indulges in it all.

To be rid of this burden of self-indulgence, go to Christ, the perfect Advocate with the Father (1 John 2:1–2). By faith hand the sins over to Him. Be specific as you confess your transgressions, and then trust in His forgiveness. He promises it (1 John 1:8–10).

If this does not bring fundamental help, ask your elders to pray for you, acknowledging your tendency to self-indulgence. At the same time, ask the Lord to search out your heart for related sins, such as daydreaming and fantasizing.

What you may learn is that the pride that keeps you daydreaming is the fundamental cause of your laziness. You may have been too proud to let the Lord search you and root out your pet sins, whatever they were. Take them seriously. Don't be afraid to grieve over them (James 4:6–10).

But be comforted. The Holy Spirit will help you (Ps. 139:23–24). Christ will write the Father's laws and love on your heart (Ezek. 36:24–25; 1 Thess. 3:5). And remember, repentance is normal for the believer, his way of responding to Christ and drawing near to the Father (Luke 15:20–24).

Sincere and swift repentance of sinful habits and attitudes can transform the ministry of the most discouraged, ineffectual pastor. Imagine for a moment a young minister who arrives at his study late, already feeling guilty because he has not begun the day in earnest prayer. Usually, the despair produced by habitual sins like these causes him to fritter away his entire time. But today he faces his sins head on. He begins his time by looking to Christ for help. He labors in prayer until he has experienced His cleansing and then seeks God's wisdom in preparing his Sunday sermon (James 1:5–8).

This time, his preparation does not consist solely of an exegesis of the passage and the writing of the sermon text. Instead, the pastor relates his calling as servant and brother to his preaching. He makes a list of several people who concern him, people he suspects may be unconverted or believers with special needs. He then takes time to pray for them.

Afterwards, he returns to the shaping of the sermon in view of the needs of the men and women for whom he has just prayed. He gives up his academic vocabulary and the elements of bookish didacticism as he thinks of their souls. Illustrations come to mind as he mentally reasons from Scripture with these lost and straying sheep. With eyes of faith he sees them—and he will have their souls for God!

By the time he leaves his study, he cannot wait until Sunday to preach. That afternoon, he puts feet on his prayers. He calls on these people to minister to them in their homes. He is becoming a person who tenderly preaches the Word in season and out. His pulpit and his study are fused into a continuum: In the study he drinks of the gospel as a thirsty sinner, and in the pulpit he pours forth the overflow to other sinners like himself (John 7:37–39).

This pastor is on his way to becoming, like Paul, a model for witness to his people. He begins by seeking the knowledge of Christ from Scripture, a knowledge which so fills him with the love of God that old sins and habits are displaced by a new fullness. Though lazy and filled with fears, he brought both failings to Christ, seeking the strengthening of his faith.

Here is our struggle: to strengthen the Christian leader by faith. "The just shall live by faith" must include the pastor's whole life, for it is this that enables him to concentrate his energies, define goals, repent of sins, and honestly face up to his own limitations. It is this that makes him a fruit-bearing disciple, eager to have answers to prayer through his own preaching, to have lives come under the power of the gospel. He is not content with a vague concept of "edification"—he prays for his hearers to be brought to a full knowledge of the Father and the Son (John 17:3). And by dealing with his own sins of pride, fear, laziness, and lust, he is able to make the message powerfully concrete.

The pastor whom God has made a model for witness is one whose character is inseparably intertwined with his faith in the gospel message. If he did not have confidence in its power to change him, the awareness of his own sins would crush his ministry. But as he leaves his idols to serve Christ, he discovers that the message purifies his heart through faith, and liberates him from all his guilty fears (2 Cor. 3:16–18; 1 Thess. 1:9–10; John 3:1–2). He is a man set free to serve a living God.

Finding the Cutting Edge

1. What is the central biblical principle for learning how to witness?
2. What happens when church officers fail to witness?
3. Charles H. Spurgeon has said that the greatest enemy of effective pastoral ministry is "officialism." By "officialism" he

meant putting yourself on a professional pedestal where what matters most of all is image and reputation. How can a pastor give up "officialism"?

4. The Good Shepherd lays down His life for the sheep; hirelings run away. The same principle applies to under-shepherds. Are you ready to die to bring lost sheep to Christ?

5. Draw up a weekly schedule showing how you think you should use your time. Then draw up a second schedule that shows how you actually use your time. The difference between the two indicates where you should be repenting.

6. The cutting edge of grace for pastors: You have heard that you can accomplish great things for God if you are willing to pray and take pains, i.e., work hard with careful attention to the details. Resolve to take pains:

   a. with your sermons, to make them bolder in content and gospel application.

   b. with follow-up of visitors to the church, using methods such as the New Life booklet or Evangelism Explosion to present Christ to the non-Christians.

   c. with your personality, to become warmer in manner and less "official" in and out of the pulpit.

   d. through recruiting people to pray for you and your ministry, aiming to get no less than fifty people praying daily for you within a year.

Notes

1. For what follows, see Carl Kromminga, *Bringing God's News to Neighbors* (Nutley, N.J.: Presbyterian and Reformed, 1976), and William Hendriksen, *New Testament Commentary, Exposition of I and II Thessalonians* (Grand Rapids: Baker, 1955), 48–57.

2. Presbyterian scholars as a rule have been slow to appreciate the magnitude of D. James Kennedy's pioneer work as expressed in his *Evangelism Explosion* (Wheaton, Ill.: Tyndale House, 1970). One of Kennedy's breakthroughs has been to point out that the New Testament presents the pastor as model and trainer who imparts knowledge on the job.

His purpose is to transform
not only individual lives but whole
cultures, and even physical creation
itself. For all of us who've heard
His voice and claim His name, Jesus'
conquest of a runaway planet
should be our main business.

—David Swartz,
The Magnificent Obsession

EIGHT

How to Involve Your Church in Evangelistic Outreach

WE HAVE SEEN THAT VISIBLE MODELS for witness are what most churches need before they can evangelize effectively. The pastor must move among his people as a shepherd who cares for them. He must let them see him witness to others. This does not mean that he must do all the work himself—not at all. But the people need to hear him present the gospel with all wisdom, fervor, and boldness.

The next step is to initiate a program involving the congregation in evangelistic outreach themselves. One that fits naturally into most church situations is one that is keyed to family hospitality and natural friendships. It can begin with a broad-based effort at friendship evangelism, in which all the families in the church are taught and encouraged to use their homes to reach out to non-Christians. From there it is a logical step for the pastor to select the more gifted and interested evangelists for further training in witnessing. These persons will be formed into a team for a more structured evangelistic outreach, including systematic calling and large-group evangelistic meetings, which could be repeated and expanded as concern for evangelism grows in the church.

This training class should be taught by someone gifted by the Spirit of God for evangelism. It may be the pastor, it may be a lay leader whose zeal for the lost has been amply demonstrated.

Before you actually begin, however, you need to make a realistic assessment of the number of trainees you can handle effectively. Do you have more than one trainer in the church? You need enough experienced people to accompany the trainees on their evangelistic appointments, especially during the early part of the program.

Perhaps you are the only one equipped to be a trainer the first time around. You may conclude that you have the resources and time to work with only one person. Don't be discouraged. It is better to choose one person who has potential as a trainer and to train him well. By so doing, you have doubled your resources. Plan to go through the course three times a year at the beginning. You'll be increasing the number of potential trainers each time around.

At the outset, the trainees should be prepared to commit themselves to one evening of group instruction per week, plus additional time (determined by the pastor or the class) for visitation and for planning the evangelistic meeting. Stress the need for consistent participation to all in the program. Otherwise the entire group loses its enthusiasm and direction because of the thoughtlessness of one or two.

The training program climaxes with a special evangelistic program. This friendship meeting can center upon a popular lecture, a ladies' tea, a prayer breakfast, a film, an open house, testimonies at a fish fry, or a discussion group. Its planning should begin early and include others besides those enrolled in the training course. If you are showing a film, the entire church should be invited to come and bring guests, help with refreshments, etc. But the specific planning needs to be done by those being trained. They are the team. Their task is to bring as many of their evangelistic contacts as possible to the special meeting. This means getting out invitations to new people as soon as possible, though without forcing the issue. It also means supplying transportation for those who need it.

One note of caution: As you develop this program and introduce it to members of your church, be careful to place it in the context of the church's broader life of witness, and the responsibility of each member to be sharing what God has done for him. You want to avoid the impression that participation in this program will fulfill one's evangelistic obligations for the next ten years! Nevertheless, this program can be helpful when presented as an introduction to organized evangelism and as a training program to equip believers to fulfill their several evangelistic responsibilities. It is an effort to heighten, systematize, and deepen what should be taking place in the local congregation.

Organizing the Evangelistic Outreach

The First Step—Prayer. The first step is to get as many people as possible praying for this outreach before it begins. The preaching that you as pastor will do in connection with it, the individuals recruited for training, the unsaved to be contacted, and the congregation's attitude toward the outreach all need to be brought frequently and earnestly to the throne of grace if you would see God's blessing.

Start by cultivating those noble people, the believing aged and shut-ins. Often they have been well trained already by the great High Priest Himself in the art of intercession. To encourage their effective prayer, be precise in explaining your goals, methods, and problems. Make your prayer requests specific, and let them know promptly what answers have been forthcoming.

Do the same at your elders' meetings. Study Acts 1–9 to show how group prayer was the basis for all church activity after the Lord's resurrection. Ask that a significant part of each official elders meeting be devoted to prayer, including prayer for the goals of the evangelism program.

Focus portions of the midweek prayer meeting on this same program. Often people do not go to prayer meeting because they do not see its importance or purpose, an attitude frequently confirmed by the widespread use of the hour as a time for Bible study instead of prayer.

Save the long Bible study for another occasion. Instead, make the Bible central in prayer meeting by following its directives for praising God and by using its promises as a basis for intercession. In prayer relate the promises of Scripture to clearly defined needs in the body, including the new emphasis on outreach.

As you do this, seek out interested people to form small prayer groups for this ministry. These groups should meet regularly and, like the other prayer warriors, should be well informed at each phase of the program.

The Second Step—Faith and Hospitality. The second step is to initiate a series of sermons on faith and hospitality. Note the combination—they must go together. Faith without hospitality withers in a vacuum of lovelessness and inactivity; hospitality without ardent faith is merely sociability, lacking the daring purpose of winning souls to King Jesus. But keep the two together, and you have a strategy blessed by God for communicating the gospel.

After the first step of praying has begun in earnest, preach three or four sermons on witness and hospitality, and conclude with a specific challenge on the use of the home in leading friends and neighbors to Christ. One evangelistic organization recommends that each family set itself an annual goal of forming a friendship with one non-Christian and winning him for Christ. Such a specific challenge provides a reasonable minimum standard for every family in the church. Some will do much more, but anyone who knows Christ at all can make one close friend in a year's time.

If this challenge is to be meaningful, however, it must not be contradicted by the example of your own home. As pastor-model, you are required by Scripture to be hospitable (1 Tim. 3:2; Titus 1:8). This is your duty and calling simply as a Christian (Heb. 13:2). Therefore, don't be taken in by the old wives' tale that pastors and their spouses cannot make personal friends. You need to explain your goals in this area to God's people and be careful not to commit the sin of partiality, but there is little justification for the notion that you should remain isolated from mankind.

The Third Step—Recruit the Gifted for Further Training. Be on the alert for the individuals who have evidenced real zeal and effectiveness in the use of their homes for witness, and ask them to take part in systematic evangelism training. There is an important spiritual principle at work here. Leadership is not arbitrarily drawn from the top; it rises as the Spirit's gifts of faith are exercised by the body of believers. Your role is that of spiritual midwife: as you assist various families in opening their homes and Bibles to friends, you seek to identify those who are being especially used by God. Ordinarily, this indicates that God is calling them to further training. Do not neglect the rest of the congregation, but for training purposes concentrate your energies here.

Begin by strengthening their faith in the power of the gospel. Give them copies of Spurgeon's *The Passion and Death of Christ*[1] and A. W. Pink's *Profiting from the Word*.[2] Spurgeon captures the power of the cross, and Pink teaches how to apply the Word to yourself with a healthy vigor. Next, show your recruits how to study the Bible, with an emphasis on personal application. Encourage them to meditate on a single chapter like Luke 6 for a month until life changes are seen in the home. Tie this to instruction on the value and power of continued confession of sin and to teaching on the importance of moment-by-moment reliance on the Holy Spirit for deepening obedience and opportunities for witness. Finally, ask them to commit themselves to training and outreach for a period of ten weeks as a minimum. An agreement to do this is important if the training is to be of any benefit to the trainees.

The Fourth Step—Systematic Calling. This phase should begin six months after your families have begun practicing evangelistic hospitality in their homes. It involves the setting up of an instruction class composed of the committed recruits you have selected, and the actual process of systematic calling on friends and neighbors (ideally, non-Christians who have experienced Christian hospitality). The first time around, two or three trainees are plenty if you do not have a supply of trainers on hand, since your students will need an experienced person to make calls with them.

If you wish, you can wait for a month before you take out class members for systematic visiting. My own instinct is to whet their appetites by taking them out right away, even though they are not yet prepared to say much. They will learn a great deal by watching you. The program outline in the next chapter sets forth the training schedule in more detail.

You want those being trained to memorize a minimum of three verses a week for the duration of the course. These verses should be chosen to deal with the holiness and love of God, the person and work of Christ, the new birth, repentance, faith, justification, sanctification, the free offer of the gospel, and the authority of Scripture.

During this training period a major goal is to equip the student with the ability to present the gospel in a simple, clear, and natural way. This requires that the pastor not insist on overloading his trainees with numerous evangelistic methods. Certainly, flexibility is a great thing, and pastors should have many evangelistic approaches. But you have years of training and experience that your students do not, so don't expect them to imitate your flexibility at this point.

Choose a method of presenting the gospel that is easily transferable. (The method set forth in these materials is that of the booklet "A New Life.") You need a bread-and-butter approach for the beginning evangelist. You can add the jam later.

During this training period you are to give instruction on the nature of the gospel and the law of God. Ask each student to write a three-minute testimony stating the main facts of the way to salvation. Have him commit this to memory and encourage him to share it right away. The governing principles are: (1) Share now and (2) Share with the people nearest to you. Begin also to take the student with you to share his testimony during your pastor calls.

Help in formulating the testimony can be found in D. James Kennedy's *Evangelism Explosion*.[3] Let the emphasis fall on three things: (1) identification of the witness as formerly self-righteous or unfulfilled, as well as blind to the love of God revealed in Christ; (2) the practical changes the gospel has brought into the life (Gal. 5:22), and the assurance of eternal life (John 3:36); and (3) praise to God for sending His Son to die for such a sinner as yourself.

The Fifth Step—The Evangelistic Evening. This is a special evangelistic program planned by the trainees and held near the close of the training program. The entire church family should be encouraged to be involved in this informal witness to non-Christian contacts. The key to the success of the program is a Spirit-imparted joy and naturalness in welcoming people. Concentrate your prayers on this goal and then determine by God's grace to have a good time yourself. Be serious about God's gospel but not grim. And do not be afraid of a touch of class if this is appropriate! Plan something that is really attractive: a film, a winsome speaker on an interesting topic, a mix of fun and games followed by testimonies and refreshments, or a program of music wisely adapted to the audience.

How should you as pastor prepare yourself for the training sessions? The most basic preparation is a spiritual immersion in the Gospel of John. You need to look at Christ through this gospel, seeing the wonder of His person and appropriating for yourself the fullness of His life. You must not merely adopt the point of view taken in the Gospel (which emphasizes the tremendous scope of the Savior's work); you must also be personally caught up in the overflowing new life that streams from Christ.

For my part, I know of no more eloquent treatment of this theme than John Calvin's exposition of John 1:14–18 in his commentary on this Gospel.[4] The commentaries on John by Leon Morris[5] and William Hendriksen[6] are also highly useful. But the best resource is the Gospel of John itself. Therefore, begin your meditation by studying the signs in the Gospel. They all focus on Christ's greatness and vital power shared with the needy through an appropriating faith.

Take as an example Christ's first miracle of turning water into wine. He does not do it on a meager scale. At a time when the wedding is nearing an end, He supplies a superabundance of the best—not to encourage drunkenness but to serve as a sign of the abundant grace available to sinners who drink of Him.

The same message is conveyed by the abundance of bread supplied to the hungry (chap. 6), the healing of the man born blind (chap. 9), and the raising of Lazarus (chap. 11). In each instance, the presence of Christ as the giver of life and light is made powerfully central by the miraculous deed. Man's response is meant to be one of immediate and total appropriation. It is this response you need to ask the Father to awaken in you. It is this response you seek to arouse in your students, and they in those to whom they witness.

Finding the Cutting Edge

1. Why was the study of the Gospel of John recommended in this chapter?
2. How many different kinds of people are confronted by Jesus in this book?
3. What different methods does He use to speak to the conscience of each? Why do you think Jesus uses so many different approaches to bring the gospel to them?
4. What social groupings are natural targets for your church? Singles? Young couples? Young people? Medical people? Retired folks?
5. Suppose you decide that singles are a promising group for your church. You have at least fifteen in your church and the singles population in your area is large. Here is a way to begin (with appreciation to Carl George for his insights). Plan a four-week series in the Sunday school hour designed for singles.
   a. *The key:* A welcoming group of singles and one or two couples commit themselves to make friends with the singles who come and to follow up with them.
   b. *The subject:* Any issue of compelling concern to singles that is stated in a positive way.

   c. *The program:*
- Arrival and refreshments (5 minutes)
- Speaker (15 minutes)
- Small group discussion (15 minutes)
- Reporting in large group (10 minutes)

   d. *The follow-up:* Use the evangelism training outlined in this chapter to follow up with the singles who respond with interest. Climax the follow-up with a singles retreat.

Notes

1. Charles Haddon Spurgeon, *The Passion and Death of Christ* (Grand Rapids: Eerdmans, 1970).

2. Arthur W. Pink, *Profiting from the Word* (London: Banner of Truth, 1970).

3. D. James Kennedy, *Evangelism Explosion* (Wheaton, Ill.: Tyndale House, 1970).

4. John Calvin, *Calvin's Commentaries, The Gospel According to St. John,* trans. T. H. L. Parker, 2 vols. (Grand Rapids: Eerdmans, 1959, 1961).

5. Leon Morris. *The New International Commentary, The Gospel According to John* (Grand Rapids: Eerdmans, 1971).

6. William Hendriksen, *New Testament Commentary, Exposition of the Gospel of John,* 2 vols. (Grand Rapids: Baker, 1953, 1954).

Caring for people is a key distinctive and quality of effective disciple-making . . . a genuine expression of God's unconditional love. . . . Effective disciple-making calls for each Christian who is a recipient of Christ's great love to become a channel through which that love can flow to those whom Christ wants to give life eternal. . . . The translation of Christ's "love" into tangible, specific action is the process of "caring" . . . spending time with a person . . . building a stronger and closer relationship . . . helping in a time of need. . . . Caring is loving, and we are called to love and care for one another.

—WIN ARN AND CHARLES ARN,
THE MASTER'S PLAN
FOR MAKING DISCIPLES

NINE

An Outline for Evangelism Training

THIS CHAPTER CONTAINS THE OUTLINE for the evangelistic training program described in the previous chapter. This ten-week
course, part of a broader evangelistic outreach involving the entire congregation, is designed to train for witness Christians
who have not had formal Bible or seminary training. However,
since it is also common for those with formal education in the
Scriptures to have missed some of the abc's of effective evangelism, this approach can serve their needs as well.

I call the approach "friendship evangelism" because of the
stress upon friendship and deeds of kindness as a foundation
for witness (Matt 5:13–16). Those participating in the training
program have already demonstrated a concern for the lost by
showing hospitality to them in their homes. The goal here is to
seek to bring the good news to people within a framework of
demonstrated Christian love. This means that a large part of this
outreach strategy involves instructing those participating on
the evangelistic opportunities that lie in all their contacts with
people, in connection with the church or elsewhere: the deacon
in his care for the sick, the poor, the aged, and the dying; the
Sunday school teacher opening his home for his students and
their families; the youth worker visiting the families of his
young people; the businessman opening his life and home to

101

his associates; and the housewife seeking out and welcoming neighbors into her home.

The training program also includes visitation evangelism, with door-to-door calling and appointments with other contacts. Even this is oriented toward the demonstration of Christ's love wherever possible. If sickness or other need is encountered in the home, those visiting should take appropriate steps to help in any way possible.

Some notes on the large-group evangelistic event called for in the course of training are in order here. The key to such an event is for it to be natural, and to put people together in a setting they can relate to without embarrassment. The evangelistic tea on a weekday morning is a natural situation for many women but not for men. Women find it normal to be invited to a neighbor's home for tea or coffee. And given the added inducement of a distinguished speaker treating a relevant topic on a popular level, they are likely to respond favorably to such an invitation. One theme that has drawn goodly numbers has been surprisingly direct: "How Jesus Christ Can Help You Be a Better Wife and Mother."

For men, the monthly or bimonthly Saturday morning prayer breakfast has proved to be attractive. Such an event consists of a rather early morning breakfast, followed by brief prayer and a well-known speaker in a church hall or local restaurant. Again, a theme that has brought positive response has been: "How Jesus Christ Can Help You Be a Better Husband and Father." The speaker must be carefully chosen. He needs some understanding of middle-class men, if that is his audience, and an ability to establish rapport with them while sharing the gospel in a winsome, practical manner. It is also important that the speaker be a man of faith and prayer so that the Spirit of God may bless this undertaking.

At evening meetings, a dinner followed by a film like "The Conversion of Colonel Bottomley" puts unbelievers at ease and yet brings into sharp focus how Christ saved a highly typical, hard-driving American man. The secret of such a meeting is to avoid hymns and the extensive use of Christian vocabulary which frightens or alienates non-Christians. Open with a simple prayer and arrange to have an informal discussion after the film of what it means to know Christ. Of course, it would be even better to have your people discuss the film with your guests on a one-to-one basis, giving the unbelievers an opportunity to respond in a casual manner.

More difficult but sometimes spectacularly effective is a discussion group format like that run by Mr. and Mrs. Bertrand Alpers in Pipersville, Pennsylvania. As new converts, they modeled their outreach along the lines of their former cocktail party encounters. Biweekly meetings were held on Friday evenings, with guests receiving a formal invitation to each affair. The invitations included a catchy statement of the subject to be discussed, which is anything from "What Is a Religious Fanatic?" to "The Happiest Day of My Life Was . . ."

When the guests arrived, they were given pencil and paper and asked to write their responses to the evening's topic. The unsigned answers were dropped into a bowl, mixed up, and then taken from the bowl and read one by one by the couple's pastor. Some were amusing, others serious. Afterwards, the minister briefly read the answer the Bible supplies to the question. Refreshments followed and the discussion continued, often beginning to break open around midnight. Typically, the last guest would leave around 3:00 A.M. Any number of conversions resulted from these casual dialogues.

A progressive dinner can also be highly effective because it is an easy way to involve a number of neighbors. But if you plan to conclude with a gospel presentation, keep it muted in tone, and let the neighbors know from the outset that you will have testimonies at some point, so that they are not left feeling that you tricked them into participating. A fish fry or barbecue also provides an appropriate setting for two or three carefully chosen testimonies to bring the evening to a climax.

(Note: On the following course outline, the chapters listed in parentheses after each "Theme" under the Weekly Instruction Period refer to the chapters in this book that deal with the topic under discussion.)

A Ten-Week Evangelistic Training Program

Week One
Memory Work
John 10:10; Galatians 5:22–23

Weekly Assignment
Reading: Psalm 67; Luke 8:26–39; Acts 8:1–8; 16:1–40

Weekly Instruction Period (One and One-Half Hours)
1. Get to know the other team members.
2. Program introduction.
3. Questions are answered and assignments made.
4. Theme: "How to Witness Through Deeds of Kindness" (chaps. 6, 8).

Outreach by Word and Deed
1. The trainer leads, and arranges appointments (accompanied by the trainee) with visitors, neighbors, and other contacts.
2. The trainee performs a deed of kindness to at least one neighbor as a basis for honoring Christ. Keep it simple.

Week Two
Memory Work
John 3:16; Romans 1:16; 3:23

Weekly Assignment
Write a three-minute testimony emphasizing knowing Christ by faith alone (chap. 8).

Weekly Instruction Period
1. Theme: "How to Talk About the Love and Power of God" (chaps. 1–3).
2. Share experiences and three-minute testimonies.
3. Introduce Fact 1 of the "New Life" booklet.
4. Begin plans for an evangelistic event. Establish a date, location, speaker, and format.

Outreach by Word and Deed
1. The trainer leads, and arranges appointments.
2. The trainee opens his or her home to a friend or neighbor for hospitality evangelism via dinner or coffee.

Week Three
Memory Work
Ephesians 2:1, 8–9

Weekly Assignment
Improve three-minute testimonies. Read half of *How to Give Away Your Faith* by Paul Little.[1]

Weekly Instruction Period
1. Theme: "How to Present the Nature of Sin from God's Point of View." Discuss Facts 2 and 3 of the New Life booklet (chap. 13).
2. Role-play going through the New Life booklet.
3. Begin a guest list for the evangelistic event, plan refreshments, etc.

Outreach by Word and Deed
1. The trainer leads, and arranges appointments.
2. The trainee pursues previous friendship contacts and visits a nursing home, with or without the trainer.

Week Four
Memory Work
Jeremiah 17:9; John 8:34; Hebrews 7:26

Weekly Assignment
Write a two-minute Christ-centered interpretation of a deed of kindness (week 1) in order to use the witness by deed as a lead-in for witness by the word.

Weekly Instruction Period
1. Theme: "How Christ Breaks the Barriers Between God and Man." Study Fact 4 of the New Life booklet.
2. Role-play using the New Life booklet.

Outreach by Word and Deed
1. The trainer leads door-to-door calling; the trainee gives his or her testimony.
2. The trainee follows up previous friendship contacts and makes new ones.

Week Five
Memory Work
Ezekiel 36:25–26; Colossians 1:13

Weekly Assignment
Read the second half of *How to Give Away Your Faith*.

Weekly Instruction Period
1. Theme: "How to Lead a Person to Christ: The Nature of Faith and Repentance." Study Fact 5 of the New Life booklet.
2. Share visitation experiences.
3. Emphasize the faith and repentance of the trainee.

Outreach by Word and Deed
1. Same as previous week.
2. Complete a list of names and addresses of those to be invited to the evangelistic event.

Week Six
Memory Work
Acts 16:31; Isaiah 55:7; 1 John 1:9

Weekly Assignment
Read Psalm 51 and Luke 15. Study the Westminster Confession and Shorter Catechism on saving faith and repentance to life.

Weekly Instruction Period
1. A test on memory verses assigned thus far.
2. Theme: "How to Help New Christians Grow in Their Knowledge of God's Love and Forgiveness."

Outreach by Word and Deed
1. The trainee takes the lead. The trainer gives his or her testimony. The trainee makes appointments.
2. Mail invitations to the evangelistic event.

Week Seven
Memory Work
John 15:16; Ephesians 1:4; Ezekiel 33:11

Weekly Assignment
Read Charles Spurgeon's *Election*[2] or R. B. Kuiper's *God-Centered Evangelism*, chapter 3.[3]

Weekly Instruction Period
1. A test on using the New Life booklet.
2. Theme: "God's Sovereignty as the Basis for Evangelism."

Outreach by Word and Deed
The trainee makes appointments, takes the lead, pursues previous contacts, and invites new contacts to the evangelistic event.

Week Eight
Memory Work
Matthew 11:28; John 7:37–38

Weekly Assignments
Read John 3, 4, 9 and Luke 7:36–50.

Weekly Instruction Period
1. Theme: "How to Use Natural Ways to Introduce the Gospel."
2. Role-playing: Guiding the conversation to Christ.

Outreach by Word and Deed
1. Continue follow-up or seek new contacts.
2. Finalize all plans for the evangelistic event.

Week Nine
Memory Work
John 15:7–8; Matthew 18:19

Weekly Assignments
Read John 15 and E. M. Bounds's *Power Through Prayer*.[4]

Weekly Instruction Period
1. Theme: "How to Pray for Your Evangelistic Outreach."
2. Discussion: Using the promises of God in prayer; the importance of praise.

Outreach by Word and Deed
1. The week of the evangelistic event: phone calls, personal visits to remind those invited to attend.
2. Event possibilities: discussion group, party, open house, film.

Week Ten
Memory Work
1 Peter 4:12–14

Weekly Assignments
Read 1 Peter.

Weekly Instruction Period
1. Evaluation of the special event.
2. Theme: "How to Teach New Converts to Witness."

Outreach by Word and Deed
Follow-up of evangelistic event contacts.

Notes

1. Paul Little, *How to Give Away Your Faith* (Chicago, Ill.: InterVarsity Press, 1966).

2. Charles Haddon Spurgeon, *Election* (Philadelphia: Great Commission Publications, n.d.).

3. R. B. Kuiper, *God-Centered Evangelism: A Presentation of the Scriptural Theology of Evangelism* (Grand Rapids: Baker, 1961).

4. E. M. Bounds, *Power Through Prayer* (Grand Rapids: Baker, reprinted 1963).

The idea of rescuing fallen humanity came from the very depths of God's eternal being. Sharing our faith in Jesus with people is to share the deep concerns of God's heart for humanity. . . . God invites us to become partners with Him; to be involved in a divine action of saving love. We are caught up in a cosmic process to redeem humanity.

—Philip Mohabir,
Worlds Within Reach

TEN

Five Steps to a Gracious Evangelistic Encounter

As you have introduced the friendship evangelism program (or some other organized program of outreach) into your church, you may have found people surprisingly willing to open their homes to non-Christians. A promising group may be prepared to take further training in evangelistic methods. But nearly all those involved (not to mention those who aren't) express concern about their ability to present the gospel calmly, clearly, and completely to their listeners. They have many unresolved fears about their ability to communicate the Christian message.

It is important for you to help them work through their fears by noting that there are different stages of witnessing, and that usually you must begin at the beginning. And that is much easier than trying to do everything at once! These stages include: preparation (friendship-building), presentation (explanation of the gospel), and follow-up (discipleship). Those being trained must not put themselves under pressure to evangelize someone with a full gospel presentation when the person is still in the preparatory stage. We should not try to force what the Holy Spirit has not yet done.

What does that mean practically? Simply that in some cases stage one is a long one, and that preparation must not be rushed. In one instance, I followed up a man with a yearly phone call or a casual visit for something like eight years before I finally presented the gospel to him in a systematic way. It came at a point of crisis in his life, and within a month this man and several members of his family were converted.

Nevertheless in many instances the preparation stage is short because the persons being evangelized have visited the church or are well known already to the witnessing Christian. Here the leader's task is to encourage those being trained just to go and "do it," that is, go with a trainer and watch his or her presentation. Then, after a time, make a presentation under the supervision of the trainer.

The point is that the Holy Spirit goes with you when you go, not when you sit and think about going.

As a pastor, you need first to remind your people that "the battle is not yours, but God's" (2 Chron. 20:15). The Holy Spirit has been given them to guide them into all wisdom and to enable them to speak the word with clarity. You might also remind them that the best way to build up confidence and expertise in communicating is by talking to people! The five basic principles of presentation which follow should provide your people with a general understanding of how to share their faith.

1. *Stick to the basics.* The first principle in effective evangelism is to preach as much of the gospel as you can without confusing or overloading the mind of the hearer. You want to give an overview of the gospel that provides the principal facts, focusing on a crucified and glorified Savior. It is this fullness of preaching that produces faith in God's elect (Rom. 10:17).

A practical implication is that it is usually better to avoid questions that lead to endless debate. Often the very reason these questions arise is the hearer's ignorance of the whole gospel system. Take the famous (and almost inevitable) question, "What about the heathen in Africa who never heard about Christ?" That question cannot be answered without explaining the whole plan of salvation. If you can get the listener to defer his questions until you have explained the entire message more fully, you will be more effective in convincing him of his own need—which at the moment is far more to the point!

2. *Recruit prayer.* Pray for yourself and recruit others to pray that you will present the gospel with the humble, gracious authority of an ambassador of Christ. God must convince you that you have a right to go to others with the gospel. It is not they who are doing you a favor to listen; you are doing them a favor to bring them this soul-transforming message. This is a matter of faith. The Devil will really attack you on this point, so guard your heart.

3. *Be clear and vivid.* Aim the message at the person and state it in language he or she can understand. The first principle of effective communication is to know what you intend to communicate and then to find the words to express it. You must develop a simple, expressive vocabulary that pictures for the listener the essential gospel truths. There is no better guide than the Scriptures themselves. They are vivid, clear, and concrete. Allied to this is the principle of necessary repetition. Expect to repeat the message in at least three different ways during a presentation if you hope to have it understood. Don't take anything for granted. Trust the Holy Spirit to apply the message, but remember that the Holy Spirit usually blesses clear speaking and thinking the most.

4. *Stress God's claims.* In all this, labor to make known the claims of God as Creator. The gospel message is what saves the person; it must have priority, therefore, in the presentation. However, make very clear to people that the law of God reveals that this is no mere projection of man's religious genius. The law shows that man is a dependent being made by God, a creature upon whom the Creator has absolute claim. God is not only our keeper; He is also our owner and master. To sin, therefore, is to be unthankful to this Creator-Master, to fight against Him with a rebellious heart, and to attempt to play God by acting as though you had independent powers of wisdom and strength. For the creature to take such a stand against the Almighty is an act of irrational madness. For this reason, Scripture often relates sin to folly and madness (Dan 4:4; Luke 15:17).

At this point your God-consciousness is of first importance. If you do not have strong convictions about the reality of a sovereign God, the absoluteness and finality of His laws, and our total dependence upon Him, it will be difficult to convince anyone else of God's claims upon them.

5. *Wait for a response.* Finally, once you have presented the whole system of truth, you must wait for the person who is listening to respond. This is difficult for talkative people to do, or for those with aggressive personalities. But it must be done. You are seeking to keep them from feeling (or actually being) psychologically trapped by a stronger personality. You are waiting for God's truth to sink in. In faith you wait on the Creator to work while you wait for the person to speak. And you are intent on seeing what this individual knows about Him. By your listening, you are really giving him or her your respect, and, most important, an opportunity to respond to God rather than to you. Here, as throughout your conversation, manners are extremely important. They are the means by which grace is made visible. Remember, the whole purpose of your presentation is to bring the person into the presence of God. And this does not happen if he or she hears you talking all the time.

Finding the Cutting Edge

1. Here are three suggestions on how to prepare yourself for witnessing more actively:
   a. Talk to your Christian friends about Christ until it is natural to speak about His great love. As you become more confident in talking about the Lord with Christians, you have trained yourself to open up about grace.
   b. Read Galatians 4:4–7; 5:6, 22–23 every morning and pray that faith will be working powerfully through love in your life and the fruit of the Spirit will abound in your relationships.
   c. Read Dale Carnegie's *How to Win Friends and Influence People.* Skills in building friendships can be used for ma-

nipulation. Avoid this. But grace expresses itself in your learning how to be gracious.

2. Pray for an increase in your alertness and intelligence in developing relationships with non-Christians. Do the following:

   a. Increase the number of your acquaintances. Slow down in your life routines; show an interest in everyone you meet.

   b. Turn already established acquaintances into friendships. The key is always showing an interest in people and their concerns.

   c. Move deeper into already established friendships by deeds of kindness and being a good listener.

3. Other possibilities: Train yourself to see the obvious. The disciples saw only a Samaritan woman at a well; Jesus saw a candidate for the kingdom. Here are possible opportunities for building friendships for witness:

   a. Identify and meet the visitors to your church. Greet them, be interested in them, ask questions that are nonthreatening. Invite them for coffee or lunch. But do not rush them.

   b. Watch for fringe people who come to your church. They may not have a living relationship with Christ. Seek them out and give your testimony when appropriate.

I cannot restrain the conviction that the reason so much confusion surrounds the Great Commission as commonly preached is just that: it is preached but not demonstrated.

—ROBERT E. COLEMAN,
THE GREAT COMMISSION LIFESTYLE

ELEVEN

Should We Evangelize the Church?

THERE IS SOMETHING TOTALITARIAN about the Lord's missionary program in the world. It requires a sold-out mind-set. Unfortunately, in the Western world the typical church member is already sold out to modern culture and its self-centered lifestyle. All he or she has to do is show up on Sunday with only occasional misses, look reasonably attentive during worship, and not forget the checkbook. No one will then question whether the church member's pre-Christian self-centeredness is still in place.

When this soft line is taken by the church and its pastors, the problem for evangelism as an enterprise is immense. We are left in the awkward position of calling people to Christ who have no clear idea of what it means to be a Christian. Here we are confronted by the strange mystery of modern apathy. Christ calls each Christian to total commitment, to soldierly participation in the work of reaching the lost, and yet we think and act in the church more like civilians in uniform.

Richard Ganz and William Edgar have pointed out the consequences of such churchly apathy in blunt language. "Evangelistic outreach is feeble," they say of the contemporary church. "Its innards eaten out . . . the church has bought and swallowed late twentieth-century culture whole."[1]

George Barna gives several clues to the depth and extent of

apathy in church members today. He writes, "This troubling state of affairs raises an intriguing question: Should we evangelize the church itself? The question is not, 'Should we evangelize the non-Christians who come to the church?' Rather, it is, 'Should we evangelize our church membership because some of these folks may not be converted?' "

I believe the answer is yes, because typically churches have members who seem to be Christians but are not. This applies to evangelicals as well as to liberals. Recently in a midwest Baptist congregation, a leading deacon went forward to receive Christ. Everyone was astonished. Here was a man who led the church, taught Sunday school, and knew all the Christian words. He said later to the pastor, "The first time I went forward to please you; this time I went forward to receive Christ for myself." Prior to this response, the man saw no reason to take Christ into his heart.

Therefore it is highly possible that a primary reason church members surrender to the American dream is the vacuum in their hearts. They surrender to the materialism of our times because no one has told them clearly that Christ loves them in the gospel and calls for immediate *surrender* to His message of mercy—not mere mental assent to its intellectual contents.

Much of the cure for our churchly materialism—and its concomitant spiritual dullness—lies with us preachers. According to Abraham Kuyper, preachers have often thought they were preaching the gospel when they were only describing it. Gospel preaching includes an imperative, and the preacher must demand the conversion of his hearers from their cultural idols. "To be free from a man's blood," Kuyper rightly enjoins us, "we must tell every man that conversion is his *urgent duty*."[2]

Keep Kuyper's concerns in mind as you lead your congregation in evangelism, for he has put his finger on a problem characteristic of many soundly orthodox churches and their leaders. Pastors tend merely to describe the gospel to their hearers, and their people generally follow the pattern in their own attempts to witness. They do not ask friends, neighbors, and their children to come to Christ. After all, they reason, is not man totally depraved and unable to come until wrought upon by the power of God? Why then ask a man to do what he cannot do?

These are good questions and deserve an answer. In fact, they *must* be answered if you hope to carry on an evangelistic outreach with any measure of conviction or power. Earlier we said that the gospel message must be aimed at men directly. Now, consider for whom we speak when approaching men with the truth. We speak for a risen Lord. We come with the royal authority of the resurrected Christ.

The way we present our message needs to reflect its authority. Sinners rarely respond to a toothless love. They ordinarily do not see any necessity for coming to the cross until they discover that it is not one option among many. They need to be shown that it is a Lion who calls them to rest on the finished work of the Lamb. As G. Campbell Morgan has pointed out, we preach the gospel of the cross from the standpoint of the risen and sovereign Lord of men and history.[3]

Therein lies our justification for a bold, confrontational presentation of the gospel of Christ. Christ the resurrected Lord commands men to repent and trust His atoning love as an urgent and solemn duty. We do not wish in any way to encourage church members to look at themselves and their sins as endless self-preoccupation. Rather our purpose is to encourage their assurance of faith by persuading them to see their sins in relationship to the transforming power of the risen Christ and His cross.

The lordship of Christ also enables us to deal with the issue of human inability in a biblical way. Often I have heard ministers and seminary students describing the unbelieving blindness of non-Christians in such a way that the unbeliever is given an excellent excuse for rejecting the message.

These evangelists are readily silenced when a man says of their exposition of the gospel, "You are right. I never thought of it before, but I can see that I am totally depraved and unable to change myself. But why get so excited? It's unfair to expect me to do anything about it. If I must die in my sins then at least I can go on and enjoy them while I live."

Such an objection shows a sinful blindness to the actual nature of human inability. It is quite true that God's sovereign grace must work first if people are to be converted. The power to turn must come from God. Because of the corruption of the human heart, people cannot by their own strength find God or even prepare themselves to do so (Gen. 6:5; 8:21; Jer. 17:9; Matt. 15:19; John 1:13; 6:37, 44; Eph. 2:1–4). But it is of crucial significance to see the particular nature of human inability. Man's *cannot* is shot through with a moral *will not*. It is not that man is a good fellow who would *like* to turn to God but is prevented from doing so by some external force alien to human nature. A person rejects Christ because his will, heart, and disposition are set against the Lord. Here we see the breaking of the first commandment and willful rejection of God's way. "All we like sheep have gone astray, and we have turned every one to his own way" (Isa. 53:6). He loves his own way and not God's service. Regrettably, his innate and inexcusable desire is to yield himself to the service of sensual unrighteousness (Rom. 6:16–18).

Our evangelism must make it clear to the sinner that this is what is happening in his life. He dare not think that his lost condition is not his concern. If you live for this present evil age, you are choosing to perish, and you are perishing because you, and you only, are rejecting God's love manifested in a blood-drenched cross. Nor must a person's inability to save himself be permitted to become a refined excuse for a stubborn refusal to come to Christ. That is why Paul reminds the Romans that knowing Christ is no great superhuman activity. We do not need to ascend to the heavens to get to Him or descend to the deep to bring Him up (Rom. 10:6–8). Instead, the word of faith (the message of the cross) brought by the preacher is on our lips and in our hearts. We simply yield ourselves in trust, believing that God raised Him up from the dead, confessing this with our mouths, and we are saved (Rom. 10:9).

The lordship of Christ means that people who keep on resisting God's grace are utterly without excuse. As the Canons of Dort note, "Men do not perish for want of an atonement." Nor must we permit them to perish without a warning.

Remember this when you are preaching, witnessing, or using the "New Life" booklet. Christ's sovereignty does not mean that we are free to force the booklet on people, but it does mean that we have a right to approach people in such a way that they are made aware that the crucified Christ is now the living Lord of glory. This living Lord expects people to bow to Him and His Word. Therefore we must expect many of them to respond as we rely on His Spirit to accomplish His work in their lives.

Notes

1. "Soldout," *Tabletalk*, April 1992, 17.

2. Abraham Kuyper, *The Work of the Holy Spirit* (Grand Rapids: Eerdmans, 1956), 353.

3. See G. Campbell Morgan, *Evangelism* (Worthing and London: Henry E. Walter, 1964), 7–24.

Because of the hostility of the devil, the work of conforming the members of Christ's body to the likeness of the soldier-image of the Head is high on the priority list of the Holy Spirit. As believers we are in Christ and He in us, and that means that His aggression against Satan must be expressed through us. So we are no longer free to play the role of civilians, living as if there were no war.

—R. Arthur Matthews,
Born for Battle

TWELVE

Revitalization Through Spiritual Inquiry

A MAJOR HINDRANCE to missionary outreach is the weakened spiritual condition of the local church. Often the typical established congregation seems permanently locked into a treadmill status quo, and even newly planted churches have a way of gradually losing their vitality as organizational demands slowly suppress the spiritual life of the body of Christ.

The discerning Baptist leader Vance Havner once said that to be a member in good standing in today's typical evangelical church, one would need to be a backslider. In his view, the contemporary "normal congregation" is miles away from the New Testament model of the church. But there is something in the picture even more deadly. Church leaders and members have often given up hope of revitalization and have lost God's vision of the harvest. There does not seem to be any way to change the situation. Many of them have made brave efforts to bring renewal to the local church, but the results have seemed negligible.

Love People Enough to Take the Heat!

However, there are ways to change the situation—if you love people enough to take the heat.

The heart of the matter is that the New Testament model of the church presupposes a greater openness in spiritual matters

123

than is normal for the modern evangelical church. In particular, the local church has given up the right to inquire closely into the spiritual condition of its members and attenders. Inquiry is assumed to be the same thing as judging from a standpoint of proud superiority. In our secularized culture, asking questions about the state of one's soul is often received as an invasion of privacy. Consequently, even the gentlest inquiry into the spiritual life of professing Christians may be misunderstood and even resented.

For example, I once asked a middle-aged woman who attended a church I served in rural Pennsylvania, "Lisa, what do you think about the change in your son's life?" The question occurred after I had shared with her how impressed I was by the transformation that had taken place in her twenty-year-old Kevin. I had made no judgment about the reality of her Christianity, but I was concerned by her apparent joylessness.

Her response was negative. "Kevin was baptized as a baby and brought up as a Christian. Why should he need a change?"

I talked to her about the new birth and conversion. I then said, "Really, it's wonderful what has happened to Kevin. He is full of joy." She did not deny the evidences of grace that now abounded in his life, but I was shocked to see how his love and joy left her cold.

Her hostility was fully unsheathed when I then inquired, "What do you think about this joy? It's certainly appealing." Then I added, with all warmth, this question: "Do you see yourself as having it?"

She dismissed me by denying my right to ask this question. I felt the steel of her hatred cut into my soul. It was such a shame that she had little interest in Christ. Was she a Christian? I did not know the answer, but her behavior made me wonder. She became my enemy for the next two years, eager to run me down in the church and the community.

The church continued to grow and two years later I left it because I could not keep up with it along with my seminary responsibilities. Soon after, a letter came in the mail. Here it is in summary form:

Dear Pastor,

Thank you, thank you, for really caring for me! I have wronged you, condemned you, judged you and spread bad reports about you. But I now have the joy you were talking about, and I cannot put in words how wonderful it is. . . . Thank you for having the courage to ask me about my joy and really about my being a real Christian. You were so right. I did not have any of it, and was very angry that you would ask about it.

While I was gossiping about you, I could not forget the question you asked me, and as time passed, I became even more joyless and haunted. Then recently I was passing by a Baptist church in nearby D——, and they were showing a Billy Graham film. I went in, listened to his message, went forward, and now I have the joy. This joy of Jesus—it's so great I can't find the words to express it. . . .

I hope my letter encourages you. Keep up your courage and don't give up on people like me.

With much joy,

Lisa

How to Build Your Own Stagnant Church

Lisa's intense, visible defensiveness is somewhat unusual among people who attend our churches. She had a background in a mainline Protestant church and apparently had been taught that baptism and church membership give you salvation. But perhaps we evangelical Christians are equally naive about the deceptions people practice within an evangelical context, often unconsciously, feeding false hopes. We need to remember that resistance to Christ can be disguised and yet inwardly be as intense as it was with Lisa.

Sin is a dark deceptive power (Heb. 3:13), and we should not be surprised that persons are drawn to Bible-believing churches without wanting their inner lives exposed by the law and the gospel. Here are five common motivations for which people identify with a church.

1. *Hunger for an emotional nest.* Some folks are seeking an emotional security blanket where they can feel safe in an upside-down world.

2. *Hunger for mental clarity.* Other people want intellectual answers in an age of incredible mental confusion. They want firm theological roots.

3. *Hunger for moral certainty.* Many desire moral certainty in a relativistic age where everyone attempts to do his or her own thing with disastrous consequences.

4. *Hunger for freedom through personal choosing.* Multitudes "choose Jesus" because they are "spiritual volunteers" who see "choosing" as a way of life. Something about Jesus appeals to their love of romance and adventure.

5. *Hunger for acceptance.* People expect that there is something they can do, or make themselves to be, to win acceptance from the church and God—through reliance on their baptism, their parents' faith, their religious experiences, and their good works.

I do not despise these longings. They can become natural bridges to lead people to hear the gospel of Christ and embrace Him by faith. But if these motivations for identification with the local church are left unexamined, then they easily become a basis for false security. Such human security inevitably keeps people from a solid knowledge of the gospel and the power it brings into the life. In this process the non-Christian inevitably interprets acceptance by the church as part of acceptance by God. Confident of their religious life, they will not see themselves as sinners needing Christ because of the peril of eternal punishment. The situation with untaught believers is much the same. They already know something of Christ, but this knowledge is hindered by all kinds of false hopes and the disappointments that false hopes bring.

Do you want to build an ingrown church? It's easy. Ignore

church members' motivations, and neglect spiritual inquiry with respect to new members and long-established ones. The downward gravitational pull of the world, the flesh, and the Devil will do the rest.

How to Stop Sending People to Hell Through Your Church

Veteran missionary and author Trevor McIlwaine says that the way to build healthy churches full of missionary life is to ask more questions about people's conviction of sin and experience of grace. He did this on the island of Palawan in the Philippines and discovered the following:

- The first missionaries led a people's movement in which thousands of islanders made professions of faith and were gathered into churches.
- The next missionaries came and discipled the people through Christian education. These missionaries assumed that the people all understood the gospel and trusted in Christ for salvation.
- McIlwaine came and asked the people many questions. What he learned was alarming. The missionaries had neglected a foundational obligation: to learn "the true spiritual condition of each person under their care."[1] The church members talked about trusting in Christ, but close listening revealed that they had not broken with the self-trust of the natural human heart.

The people were still trusting in their good works, prayers, repentances, and church membership as their eternal hope, and instruction in discipleship simply frustrated them and left them guilt-ridden.

Here is McIlwaine's sad conclusion: "They had been instructed to live like Christians, but many were not children of God. Had they not been alerted to their grave danger, they would have gone on in this condition to a lost eternity."[2] There is no room here to explore the careful way in which he came to his conclusions, but his warnings are sobering. He also applies them to the home church. In effect, he says that the members and leaders of the local church need to stop sending people to hell, leaving non-Christians with a false sense of security.

He appeals for more searching preaching as part of the cure, and for more church members to involve themselves with soul care. In his view we must not let ministering to "felt needs" crowd out the biblical vision of heaven and hell. McIlwaine cited the time when he was preaching a series of messages in an evangelical church and an elderly man approached him. He said, "I am in deep trouble." The trouble turned out to be that the man had been a member of the church for forty years but now admitted, "I do not know the Savior." The preaching had disturbed the man, and he apparently became a Christian because he now understood he was in danger of eternal condemnation. But "though some fellow church members had wondered if he was saved, they had never questioned him."[3]

How Do You Graciously Talk About the Absence of Grace?

But how do you do this work? If you take your responsibility to care for souls seriously, will you not risk making grave mistakes through haste and thoughtless enthusiasm? The answer is yes. One danger is that the pastor or church member engaged in this task may rashly identify people as lost or saved and do so in a judgmental manner. As Jonathan Edwards warned in his study of revivals, hasty judgments about people's eternal destiny are risky and often wrong. The cautions of this wise man are a good check on our attempts to evaluate people by our own fleshly wisdom.

Therefore the best way to begin this work is to humble yourself and taste afresh of the grace of God (James 4:6–10). Humbling only comes through a better knowledge of the law and the gospel. The law shows us the depth of our sin and desert of hell, and the gospel shows us the depths of God's grace. We learn from Jesus' substitutionary suffering what hell is like and what an immeasurable burden our sin was to carry. As we reflect upon the depth of our own sins, as we carefully recall how once we hated God, we are renewed in the knowledge of the present value of the message of the cross. Our joy abounds as we grow in our deep gratitude for His love. Certainly, justification by faith is once-for-all, but we need fresh applications of the blood of Christ for our daily forgiveness (1 John 1:1–2:2). Accordingly our biggest need is to stay daily in touch with what we once were, to wake up to how much the flesh is still a power in our lives, and how spiritual vitality depends upon frequent confession of our sins. We must not lose touch with our unworthiness and the inexpressible love of the Savior for us.

So taste the joy of a deepening repentance! Then the communication always improves, and we are soul doctors who do not neglect our own souls. We listen so much better, and we are deeply sympathetic, yet we are also deeply committed to the truth. We are not willing in any way to offer false comfort to people who still trust in their own merits and not in Christ's.

Given this stance, we find that our very joy becomes a convicting power in the lives of church members and attenders who are resisting grace. Our aim in helping others to a God-centered self-understanding is not to encourage morbid introspection, but to lead wanderers to taste of heaven's joys with us.

One way to put feet on this approach is to build a relationship with someone and ask what can be called "soul questions." Here are some questions I have used that have brought people to conversion and believers to a renewed experience of grace:

- Have you ever stopped doing a single thing because you love Jesus?
- Have you ever started doing a single thing because you love Jesus?
- Do you enjoy prayer? Do you enjoy Christians?
- What is the gospel? Does it give you great joy?

- Do you regularly forgive others?
- Do you have any sense that your own sins are forgiven?
- Do you recall your conversion to God? How were you different afterwards?

Finding the Cutting Edge

1. Often grace and the message of the cross mean little to people because they have no understanding of their peril. God is seen as a genial Santa Claus who has no wrath toward sin. And they see themselves as basically good people who pretty much deserve heaven. To tell them, "Jesus died for you," sounds nice and comforting, but why did He go to all the trouble? To get the idea straight, complete this story based upon one in James Denny's *The Death of Christ.*

   "A man is sitting on a pier fishing on a calm summer day. Suddenly another man comes running down the pier, dives into the water, and drowns. Having witnessed this, I explain to the fisherman, 'This man died for you!' The fisherman, however, has great trouble understanding why the man needed to die for him. After all, he was in no danger that he could see."

   Now, rewrite the story so that the fisherman can see that he is in peril and has a desperate need.
2. James Denny says that the parable of the fisherman unaware of his peril reflects the way modern evangelists and pastors often present the gospel. They minimize human depravity, and so the preaching of the cross loses its power. The human predicament is seen as more psychological than judicial before a holy God. With that in mind, why is such a weak evangelism so popular today?
3. Meditate on Ezekiel 33 as a way of catching God's burden for the lost. Then make this chapter a basis for prayer in behalf of several people you would like to ask about their souls.
4. Ask at least five people to pray for your tenderness to increase as you go about this work.

Notes

1. Trevor McIlwaine, *Building on Firm Foundations* (Sanford, Fla.: New Tribes Mission, 1991), 1:20.

2. Ibid.

3. Ibid.

Apart from the special, saving grace of God, people are dead in sin, darkened in their understanding, alienated from the life of God and hardened in heart (Eph. 2:1; 4:18). And the means God has ordained to administer that special saving grace is the preaching of the gospel of Jesus Christ.

—JOHN PIPER,
DESIRING GOD

THIRTEEN

How to Witness with the *"New Life" Booklet*

BECAUSE OF ABUSES both real and imagined, many Christians have little use for tracts and "witnessing booklets." In particular, they fear a mechanical approach to the Christian witness that minimizes person-to-person contact. They also rightly suspect that brief written summaries can truncate the gospel or be used to bring about hasty "decisions" that have nothing in common with biblical conversion.

These dangers are real enough. But they can be avoided by careful submission to the principles found in the Word of God. When this submission governs our approach, we discover that written materials are greatly used of God in clarifying the gospel, first for ourselves, and then for those to whom we speak. If properly developed, such evangelistic instruments can provide a comprehensive picture of the Christian faith, an overview introducing non-Christians to the broad sweep of Christian teaching. This has great advantages because many unbelievers have completely erroneous conceptions of the Christian faith.

Likewise, such presentations help witnessing Christians to see Bible doctrines from the standpoint of Scripture's evangelical center. They balance the Christian by almost forcing him to subjugate his own "pet" doctrines to the presentation of the gospel as a whole. One person may tend to focus on sin and the law of God, another on Christ and God's mercy, and yet another on the conversion experience. All this is fine, but we must not make one aspect of truth the whole truth, especially when we present the gospel.

Within Reformed circles this need for balance is especially pressing. Our recent history has been all too often one of reaction against Arminianism and semi-Arminianism. As a consequence, many Reformed pastors have virtually dropped the preaching of the cross from their pulpit ministry. And Reformed people as a whole hesitate to tell people about the death of Christ for fear of falling into a man-centered approach to the lost.

I am convinced that a witnessing guide based upon sound biblical theology can avoid the dangers described and help Christians to offer a God-centered presentation of the gospel to the lost. Not the least of its value is the fact that a well-written tract can also function as an icebreaker, a natural way to get into a serious conversation about very personal matters. This is especially important because some Christians just do not know how to engage unbelievers in conversation about the things of Christ.

A tract or booklet does not need to be thrown at strangers like a hand grenade into an enemy camp. One person wisely noted that it functions best as an extension of your arm. It is a tool to be used in a highly personal way—warmly, graciously, and wisely, with complete reliance on the Holy Spirit.

It is for such use that the booklet "A New Life" has been prepared (see Appendix). Its stress falls on the Christian message as the personal gospel of hope for men trapped in their sins and miseries. Without in any way compromising the particularity of Christ's atonement, the booklet emphasizes the personal love of God for sinners, the availability of grace for men in their lost condition, and the power of the gospel to meet them where they are.

What follows is an outline of the "New Life" booklet to help the Christian develop a detailed understanding of the way it presents the gospel. Familiarity with its structure will greatly enhance a free and natural presentation.

Jesus' method of witnessing in John 4 provides the basic outline for the booklet. He begins by calling attention to Himself as the gift of God, the source of a supernatural life for mankind (John 4:10, 14). Afterwards He speaks to the woman about her sins in a very particular way (vv. 16–18). But He focuses first on the grace of God, and only within this context does He draw attention to the law of God.

Here the gospel of hope provides the controlling framework, and the doctrine of man's sin is presented within this particular structure. Condemnation thus can be of the severest sort when properly related to the gospel message. But exposure of sin apart from God's mercy rarely brings sinners to repentance.

Fact 1: A loving God sent His Son, Jesus, into the world to bring you to a new and abundant life.

There are two aims here. First, the intention is to show that God's purpose toward the world is to save it. The world is already under condemnation because of its unbelief, but Jesus has been sent by the Father to save.

Hence, God's purpose in the gospel is positive (John 3:17; 1 Tim. 1:15). It is good news for those who of themselves deserve only the bad news of eternal wrath.

Second, the intention is to stress the power and fullness of Jesus' person and work in dealing with people's sins and miseries. A normal Christian life is one in which empty sinners become full through the daily drinking of Christ.

Thus the gospel is a message of hope both in God's saving intention toward sinners, and God's saving power for sinners.

Fact 2: People are self-centered, not God-centered.

Here we introduce the idea of sin in words understandable to contemporary people. It is presented as an attitude, or a state of mind, in rebellion against the Creator. In his rebellion man as a creature centers his life on himself and not on God. This self-centered outlook is called being "dead in trespasses and sins" (Eph. 2:1). It expresses itself in dependent man proclaiming his independence of his Maker. This blindness is named "The Big Lie."

Since this self-centered life contradicts reality, man finds himself and his societies torn by the vicious habits and acts that are described in Romans 1:21–32 and listed in the booklet (see Appendix). These outworkings of man's self-deception point him to the deeper cause of his sorrows—his rejection of his dependent creaturehood. What we want him to see is that the root of his problems lies in his denial of the Creator's total claim on him as a creature made in His image. People today are accustomed to taking each religious system as just one more set of interesting opinions, and need to be faced with God's absolute claim on every person as the Owner of all. Man needs to know that God has made him and has a right to call him to repentance for his self-centered life.

Fact 3: Self-centered man is separated from a Holy God by three big barriers.

Here sin is presented from God's point of view. Three wide barriers of sin—a bad record, a bad heart, and a bad master—separate God and man. God has a holy refusal to meet with man, and man, an unholy refusal to meet with God. That is, a holy God cannot come to man without a removal of the three barriers of man's unholiness. Man refuses to come to God because he loves his sin and hates God.

As a consequence, God has a "problem" with man's sin in that He cannot pardon it without a just basis, a proper ground. It is not a problem in the sense of God's being frustrated or helpless, but He is not free to forgive and cleanse men of sin without a mediator. And man left to himself can only receive the wages of sin that he has earned, namely, eternal death.

Fact 4: God's solution! No barriers!

God's solution to the problem of sin is to introduce a perfectly righteous Mediator, Jesus the God-man, who breaks through the three barriers of sin and brings God and man together. His righteousness enables a holy God to justify the ungodly (Rom. 4:5).

Observe carefully that the Lord Jesus supplies everything sinful man lacks: a perfect record for a bad record, a new heart for a bad heart, and Himself as a good Master for the bad mastery of sin.

The Son of God accomplishes this by becoming the substitute man, the righteous representative of sinners, who goes to the cross in the place of His people. He dies in the culmination of a life of perfect obedience and service to God. Unrighteous man had earned eternal death, but now a righteous Man earns eternal life for His own sheep and gives it as a free gift to those who believe.

Fact 5: How to receive the Lord Jesus into your life.
In this section the sinner learns what God expects of him. He is told that he may have salvation *now* by turning from his sins and trusting in Jesus alone as Lord and Savior.

Be careful at this point, for man's natural bent is to center on himself, and he will likely think of his repenting and believing as something he does apart from Christ. This is a grave mistake and produces religious experience that is largely psychological. Therefore stress that repenting and believing is God's appointed way of coming to Christ, and that Christ alone does the saving.

Begin a New Life. In this section, the person going through the booklet is challenged to respond to what he has learned about Christ and God. The prayer is a guideline for the man who wishes to receive Christ, but it must not be presented as a magical guarantee that anyone will be automatically saved by praying it. Afterward, the man should not be given assurance that the mere offering of a prayer saves him.

However, Scripture does promise that whoever calls upon the name of the Lord will be saved (Rom. 10:13). Therefore the man who sincerely calls upon God to save him using this prayer or his own words will, in fact, find God ready to do so.

Since salvation begins in prayer, the booklet strongly urges upon the new believer the need to pray continually. Prayer, broadly understood, is presented as the central and distinguishing feature of the Christian life. Bible reading and Bible study are also presented as steps in obedience to the resurrected Lord. The person who has trusted in Jesus has a secret resurrection life (Col. 3:1–4), and it is to be expected that he now has the power from the Lord to put his sins to death (Col. 3:5–11).

The emphasis on worship in a scripturally directed church is combined with a call for meditation on God, His world, and our place in it. The purpose here is to challenge the new disciple to begin to think in a Christian manner about all areas of life and to see his Father's hand in everything that comes to pass.

Encourage the new convert to witness in a natural, kindly way to friends and relatives. He should remember that shortly before, he too was blind to the great mercies of God. Especially discourage witnessing in pride and with any idea that the disciple has new life or power apart from Christ.

Getting Started. Now you are ready to share the booklet with others. Do you find yourself hesitating? All your friends and neighbors suddenly seem self-sufficient. Why would they want to hear about Christ?

Wait a moment! Don't abandon evangelism before you even begin! Don't try to choose the elect! That happens to be God's task. How do you know whom God will call to Himself? God has a sovereign plan conceived in all wisdom. In that plan He brings you to the people He wants you to meet. Is it not likely that He will be guiding you to His own sheep among your friends? Be a friend with a difference. Be more friendly than you ever were before and prepare yourself to witness by taking the following steps:

1. Pray before you go with the gospel, asking God to prepare both you and the person you meet. Make an essential part of this prayer a specific request for humble, loving boldness. The gospel is a message having God's own authority. If you act and speak as though you were not a messenger of the great King, then you are a virtual contradiction to what you are saying.

In practical terms, this means you must believe that you have a right to bring the gospel to others. Those who listen to you are not doing you a favor; you, rather, are doing them a favor. Keep this in mind especially when you are discouraged by opposition and conflict.

Develop some natural introductions for presenting the "New Life" booklet. A natural introduction can be very effective when you yourself are enthusiastic about the booklet.

One opening might be: "Have you seen the booklet called 'A New Life'? It's really meant a lot to me, and I'd like to share with you some of the things I've learned from it."

Another might be: "You know, George, a lot of people have been looking at this booklet called 'A New Life.' I have a copy of it here which you can take with you. After you read it, let's get together and talk about it."

Again, "Mary, you said you couldn't believe the Bible. I can understand your problem. But have you ever really gotten an overview of what the whole Bible is about? It certainly wouldn't be fair to yourself or to the Scriptures if you didn't take a little time to consider the central message of the Bible. You can catch something of the broad picture through a little booklet I have here."

2. Start using the booklet immediately. Simply take your pen and circle the main words and draw arrows to the principal thoughts. At times this will seem absurd and useless. But fight off the thought that your listener isn't paying attention. Be enthusiastic about Christ's love and tremble as you consider the awfulness of man's sin. You can be sure that most people will listen then.

3. Be thoroughly familiar with the booklet yourself. Memorize the Scriptures cited and study the connections between the various facts. For example, the relationship between Facts 1 and 2 is that of contrast. Therefore, emphasize the difference between the new life given by the Spirit as set forth in Galatians 5:22 and the state of man described in Ephesians 2:1–3.

Facts 3 and 4 are related to each other as problem (Fact 3) and solution (Fact 4). Sin is the problem; Christ is the solution. Bring this out as you go.

Especially note the question under "Begin a New Life": "Will you now surrender your life to Christ by turning from your self-centered way and trusting in Him alone?" Ask it, then wait until the person responds. In many instances the person will say that he hopes to be accepted into heaven on the basis of God's general kindness and his own good works. If you get this answer, turn back to Facts 3 and 4 and go over the three barriers again, and Christ's work as Mediator in removing them.

Similarly, in going over Fact 5, I often find it helpful to turn again to Fact 4 and relate faith to Christ's breaking the barriers.

Try to move through the booklet at a good pace. You can always come back and go through the booklet a second or third time. But I usually try to cover most of the five facts in about 30 minutes. The reason for this rate of speed is to give the person an overview of the whole message in a rather short time, and to keep from getting sidetracked so that the booklet doesn't get covered. (This half hour, of course, does not include the time spent on "How Does This New Life Continue?")

Remember, faith is the motivational force for Christian witness. And you get more faith as you seek it by prayer and earnest Bible study. Thus you go to the work of evangelism with a seriousness and a determination wrought by the Holy Spirit.

However, faith often seems to be at its lowest ebb just before you go forth with the message. Satan may shower the believer with doubts at such moments. But then as you go, you are astonished to see how faith and joy begin to abound.

Why? The answer is that God gives the Holy Spirit "to those who obey him" (Acts 5:32), and going with the gospel is one of the many ways in which the believer expresses his obedience as a disciple (Matt. 28:16–20; 2 Cor. 5:20). "And I tell you, everyone who confesses me before men, the Son of man will confess before the angels of God; but he who denies me before men will be denied before the angels of God" (Luke 12:8–9).

The essence of faith is to come to Christ. This is the first and the last and the surest indication that faith is still alive. A sinner has nothing but sin and distress. . . . Faith manifests itself clearly and plainly when sinners, instead of fleeing from God and their own responsibility, as they did before, come into the presence of Christ with all their sin and all their distress. The sinner who does this believes.

—Ole Hallesby,
Prayer

Fourteen

Mobilizing Through Faith: God's Way to Do God's Work

EVERY ATTEMPT TO COUNSEL A PASTOR on mobilizing his congregation for witness (including this one) fills his mind with admonitions and suggestions regarding his task. I would like to end this book with a reminder of what his task is *not:* He has *not* been called to create the mandate for evangelism, nor must he provide the spiritual power to carry it out. The Lord of the church is the one who has furnished both the mandate and the means for her global witness. We might say that we do not create Pentecost; Pentecost creates us. We are part of God's new creation, joining with Christ as He extends the spread of new life around the globe. All that is asked of us is that we lay hold of Christ in such a way that our lives are daily transformed to share the mind, power, and heart of the Lord Jesus.

In his commentary on John 1:16, Calvin discusses how the fullness of God is available to the believer: "In Christ the wealth of all these things is laid before us that we may seek them in Him. Of His own will He is ready to flow to us, if only we make way for Him by faith."[1] Note Calvin's last clause. It is faith alone that lays hold of Christ's fullness for us, at the moment of our conversion and through our Christian life. Without faith, what we have learned of Christ's practical sovereignty will be useless to us. We will lack the power of Christ to undertake our ministries. What we need, then, is to understand the nature of

143

faith and how it appropriates Christ's fullness for our lives and witness.

From the moment of our justification, the function of biblical faith is to receive from Christ what we lack in ourselves. We receive God's salvation when we abandon our own efforts and claim Christ's righteousness as our own by faith in His work for us. Faith is God's gift (Eph. 2:8–10); it is the means He uses to transfer His fullness and life to us. When faith is properly exercised, God bestows on us what once belonged solely to Him— perfect righteousness, the Holy Spirit, the fruits of the Spirit, etc. The windows of heaven are opened wide to the person whose arms are spread out in faith!

Because that is so, the Scriptures go on to affirm that faith can indeed do marvelous things. Perhaps the most astonishing passage on the subject is Mark 9:23: "All things are possible to him who believes" (NASB). Our familiarity with this verse has done much to weaken the impact of its promise, but the words hit us with renewed force when we realize that ultimately it is of God alone that we can say, "All things are possible to *Him.*" Men and angels certainly lack that power in themselves, yet God, through Christ, promises *all power* to our faith. What Christ is actually saying is that faith, in its receptive, appropriating character, receives God Himself! It has nothing to do with man's moral achievements or intellectual strivings. Faith is a dependence on Christ's indwelling that Scripture variously describes as "looking," "seeing," "coming," "resting," "receiving," and even "eating" and "drinking."

This amazing truth should help us to see many things more clearly. For one, it should help us understand the missionary failure of so many congregations today. Plainly, God would have us see that all the resources have been available for accomplishing the deeds of God. What has failed is our appropriating faith. The promises of God have gone unclaimed, with no one to embrace them as their own, and the church has more and more retreated into her protective shell.

If that is the case, what can we do about it? The cure for this grave sin of unbelief is to get back to the Scriptures as God's missionary epistle setting forth His vision of mercy in Christ. We need to read the Bible in a new way: to claim its promises as the personal commitments of our loving Father, and to receive its directives to the New Testament church as directives to us as well. The result would be a witness of such boldness and commitment that cultists would blush over their comparative lack of zeal!

One more question remains. We have seen that faith is what we need to receive the fullness of God into our lives, but how exactly is this accomplished? It is through prayer that faith reaches out to Christ and His abundance of grace. In this communication with our heavenly Father, our hearts are softened and attuned to the missionary nature of God. Through prayer God brings the severity of the law and the dreadful fate of the lost home to our understanding. He gives us a fresh awareness of the wonder of His gift to the world in Christ. And it is through prayer that the New Testament picture of a vital, witnessing church comes alive. We receive the mind, the heart, and the power of Jesus Christ.

God uses the prayer of faith to bring the fullness of Christ into our churches and our lives, for when we pray, our faith becomes daring through the power of love. The "faith that works by love" (Gal. 5:6) enables its possessor to fulfill the command to love your neighbor as yourself (5:13–14) and to walk in the Spirit and put to death the works of the flesh (5:16–26). The verb translated "works" in verse 6 has in it the idea of unusual energy, even supernatural power. Clearly, God is eager to perform His works through us. Let us claim, with great anticipation, Paul's prayer as our own: "Finally, brethren, pray for us, that the word of the Lord may speed on and triumph, as it did among you" (2 Thess. 3:1 RSV).

Notes

1. John Calvin, *Calvin's Commentaries, The Gospel According to St. John,* trans. T. H. L. Parker (Grand Rapids: Eerdmans, 1959), 1:23.

APPENDIX

A New Life

Have you ever felt there was something missing in your life? Something important but you didn't know what? That may be the **new life** God wants you to have. A life of joy, peace, and fulfillment. A life . . . which you can receive today. Carefully consider these **Five Important Facts** . . . and find out how you can get that new life and become a brand-new person.

1. A loving God sent His Son Jesus into the world to bring you a new and abundant life.

> Jesus said: "If anyone thirsts, let him come to me and drink. He that believes in me . . . from within him shall flow rivers of living water" (John 7:38–39).

> He also said concerning those He loves: "I came that they might have life and have it abundantly" (John 10:10).

This new life brings you the fruit of the Spirit: "love, joy, peace, patience, kindness, goodness, faithfulness, gentleness, self-control" (Galatians 5:22). **It also gives POWER!**

God's Holy Spirit gives you the power to overcome . . .

> feelings of loneliness, stress, fear of people and the future (1 John 4:18).

And the power to break unbreakable habits like . . .

> selfishness, depression, uncontrolled anger, prejudice, sexual lust, overeating, overdrinking, drug abuse (1 Corinthians 6:9–11).

But why are so many people without this new life?

2. *Because . . . people are self-centered, not God-centered.*

This means that by nature you are spiritually dead and deceived. (Ephesians 2:1: "You were dead through your trespasses and sins.")

TO BE SPIRITUALLY DEAD AND DECEIVED is to be centered on yourself and not on your Creator, and to believe . . .

A Big Lie

People show this according to Romans 1:21–31 by being . . .

> unthankful to God, perverted, greedy, jealous, bitter, proud, mean, devious, foolish.

Since man's first sin, he has tried to be INDEPENDENT of God. Actually each human being is entirely DEPENDENT on God for breath, food, health, shelter, physical and mental abilities. THE BIG LIE: SELFISH INDEPENDENCE:

> self-trust, self-boasting, self-reliance, self-analysis, self-hating, self-seeking

3. *Self-centered man is separated from a holy God by three big barriers.*

Bad record
Romans 3:23
"All have sinned . . ."

Bad heart
Mark 7:21
"From the heart of man come evil thoughts . . ."

Bad master
John 8:34
"Whoever commits sin is a slave . . ."

. . . consequences of sin as separation from God. "The wages of sin is death" (Romans 6:23a).

Now
1. A dry, thirsty, unsatisfied life.
2. A guilty, accusing conscience (depression, fears, etc.).
3. An aging body that must shortly die.

To Come
1. Loss of all friendship and earthly joys forever (Matthew 8:12).
2. Frightful pains of body and conscience forever (Mark 9:48).
3. Dreadful thirst of soul and body forever (Luke 16:19–31).

4. God's Solution! No Barriers!

Perfect Record
1 Corinthians 1:30
"Christ . . . is made our righteousness."

New Heart
Ezekiel 36:25–26
"A new heart I will give you."

Good Master
Matthew 11:28–30
"My yoke is easy."

"The blood of Jesus, God's Son, cleanses us from all sin" (1 John 1:7)

The benefit of Jesus' death . . . Love's Biggest Gift
"The free gift of God is eternal life through Jesus Christ" (Romans 6:23). Jesus the God-man is the biggest gift of the Father's love. On the cross Jesus suffered all the torments of hell as a substitute for His people (John 3:16; 10:15). He was legally condemned by God as their representative, removing the barriers

of a bad record, a bad heart, and a bad master. The Father's love can do no more. Risen from the dead, Jesus now lives to give you a new record, a new heart, Himself as a new master—and the free gift of eternal life now!

You Need to Make Sure:

> God says you either have a NEW LIFE or you are a law-breaker DEAD in your self-centeredness. Are you personally alive or dead? If you are still dead, you need to know . . .

5. *How to receive the Lord Jesus into your life . . .*

1. Turn

> in sorrow from your sins: "Let the wicked forsake his way, and the unrighteous man his thoughts; let him turn to the LORD, that He may have mercy on him, and to our God, for He will abundantly pardon" (Isaiah 55:7).

2. Trust

> in Christ Jesus alone: "Believe in the Lord Jesus Christ and thou shalt be saved, and thy house" (Acts 16:31).

Repentance is . . . not our suffering or our good works to earn our salvation, but a turning from our sins to the living God through Jesus Christ.

Trust in the Lord Jesus is . . . accepting, receiving, and resting on Him alone as the Savior from our sins.

Begin A NEW LIFE

Will you now surrender your life to Christ by turning from your self-centered way and trusting in Him alone? Here is a guideline to help you confess your sins and come to know God through taking the Lord Jesus Christ as your *own* personal Savior:

"Heavenly Father, I am really a selfish person. I have wanted my own way—not yours. I have often been jealous, proud, and rebellious. You are my Creator, but I have acted as though I was lord of all. I have not been thankful to you. I have not listened to your Word the Bible and have not loved your Son. But now I see that all my sin is against you. I now repent of this evil attitude. I turn from all my sins and trust that Jesus shed His precious blood to cleanse me from all my guilt. I now receive Him as my Savior and Lord of my life."

I, _____, turn from my sins and take Christ as my Lord and Savior. By His help I promise to obey Him in every part of my life.

How Does This New Life Continue?

The same way it began—in faith and prayer.

1. Pray constantly . . . Prayer is talking to God. Keep doing it all the time. Include in it praise, thanksgiving, confession of sins, petitions for others' salvation, and requests for help.
2. Read your Bible . . . Study your Bible every day. It is the food for your new life and your sure guide. In it you meet Jesus and learn to claim His promises for your life.
3. Worship with others . . . Meet with a church where the Bible is taught and obeyed and where Jesus Christ is Lord and Savior.
4. Witness to others . . . Tell your friends what Christ has done for you—and wants to do for them. Be tactful and back up your words by improvement in manners and doing deeds of kindness.

Additional copies of this booklet are available through:

World Harvest Books and Tapes
Call toll-free 877-255-9907

Or visit our website at:
www.whm.org